D1036814

Creating the High-Performance Team

Creating the High-Performance Team

Steve Buchholz, Ph.D.
Thomas Roth
Wilson Learning Corporation

edited by
Kären Hess, Ph.D.

John Wiley & Sons, Inc.
New York • Chichester • Brisbane • Toronto • Singapore

Publisher: Stephen Kippur
Editor: David Sobel
Managing Editor: Andrew Hoffer
Editing, Design & Production: Publications Development Company

This publication is designed to provide accurate and authoritative information in regard to the subject matter covered. It is sold with the understanding that the publisher is not engaged in rendering professional advice. If professional advice or other expert assistance is required, the services of a competent professional person should be sought.

Copyright © 1987 by John Wiley & Sons, Inc.

All rights reserved. Published simultaneously in Canada.

Reproduction or translation of any part of this work beyond that permitted by Section 107 or 108 of the 1976 United States Copyright Act without the permission of the copyright owner is unlawful. Requests for permission or further information should be addressed to the Permissions Department, John Wiley & Sons, Inc.

Library of Congress Cataloging-in-Publication Data

Buchholz, Steve.
Creating the high-performance team.

Bibliography: p. 185
Includes index.
1. Work groups. 2. Industrial organization.
I. Roth, Thomas. II. Hess, Kären. III. Wilson Learning Corporation. IV. Title.
HD66.B82 1987a 658.4'02 86-32623
ISBN 0-471-85672-X
ISBN 0-471-85674-6 (pbk.)

Printed in the United States of America

87 88 10 9 8 7 6 5 4 3 2 1

Contributors

D. L. Barkemeyer
Dow Chemical
Midland, Michigan

John King
Wilson Learning Corporation
Glendale, California

George Land
Leadership 2000
Paradise Valley, Arizona

Velma Lashbrook
Wilson Learning Corporation
Eden Prairie, Minnesota

Michael Leimbach
Wilson Learning Corporation
Eden Prairie, Minnesota

Larry Wilson
Pecos River Conference Center
Santa Fe, New Mexico

C. T. Mok

Contents

ᵌᵒᴹ·T·ᵕ

Introduction

What is a high-performance team? To answer this critical question, Wilson Learning Corporation worked with a significant number of Fortune 100 clients, to find out what their answers would be. These clients represent many different types of groups, fixed-work groups, quality circles, and matrix groups. By examining these diverse team applications and listening to managers and workers describe peak experiences, the authors isolated specific attributes characteristic of high-performance teams.

Hughes Aircraft co-partnered a concerted effort to develop a learning methodology to create a high-performance team. One application of that methodology is a prominent seminar participated in by thousands of managers nationwide. A second application of the methodology is a process for using the high-performance team to solve business-related problems. Another application is the examination of organizational transformation. How can an organization which operates primarily through individual initiative be transformed into one which uses a cooperative approach?

The team approach is not new. Quality circles, for example, have been in existence for several years as one kind of team approach. Many have not accomplished the hoped-for results, however, for several reasons. Often only a small percentage of the work unit is included. Typically the groups' actions are viewed as an event rather than as a way of life or a philosophy of management. New programs come and go and can easily be viewed as fad management. The team approach must become a management philosophy, permeating the entire work culture, rather than an approach that is unusual or out of the ordinary.

The quality circle or "program" approach is analogous to a heart transplant in that a new program is brought into the culture without taking steps to change the culture or "prepare the soil." It is likely that the culture will reject the new addition just as a body often rejects a new organ. If only one or two hours of a forty-hour week use the team approach, the approach is likely to have limited impact.

Another reason for the failure of some quality circles is that many managers lack the beliefs and skills needed to lead a team. Further, team members are not used to relating cooperatively; many lack the required trust and interpersonal skills to function as team members. What is needed is an on-going process of team development—a basic premise of Wilson Learning.

The Purpose of This Book

Creating the High-Performance Team (*CHPT*) provides you with the one-to-group skills needed to:

- Provide strong leadership
- Create and reinforce a positive work culture
- Create and gain alignment on a departmental purpose
- Lead your team to interdependence and group synergy
- Create meetings characterized by high communication and trust
- Encourage employees to use their creative talents
- Solve problems
- Recognize and define opportunities
- Gain team commitment

An Overview

Chapter 1 examines what constitutes a high-performance team and how the management skills needed to deal with such a team differ from traditional one-on-one management skills. Chapter 2 examines the type of leadership most effective for high-performing teams and how the role of manager has shifted over the past decade. Chapter 3 examines the transformation from manager-held responsibility to group-held responsibility and how the group might be encouraged to accept such responsibility. Chapter 4 looks at the importance of group involvement in and commitment to an overall departmental purpose.

Chapter 5 deals with factors critical to a high-performance team: effective two-way communication, a willingness to communicate, and a way to deal with conflicts that occur. Chapter 6 looks at motivation, the willingness to change, and the ability to focus on the future. Chapter 7 examines ways of increasing the effectiveness of meetings and keeping the group focused on task. Chapter 8 discusses ways that managers limit their own creativity and that of their employees and how such barriers to creativity can be overcome. Chapter 9 introduces a method for identifying opportunities and ways for responding rapidly to them. Chapter 10 reviews the attributes of a high-performance team and identifies areas where you can begin to create such a team with your own work unit.

The Payoff

As you use what you have learned in this book, you should experience:

- More efficient, effective use of your time and energy
- Increased comfort level dealing with groups
- Increased communication within your work unit
- Shared ownership for performance results of your work unit.

Throughout the book you will be asked to look at traditional assumptions about managing and to think about the possibility for change in your organization. As noted by Charles H. Brower, "Change is what makes the world go round, not love—love only keeps it populated."

Two heads are better than one

—John Heywood

Wearing the same shirts doesn't make you a team.

1

What Is a High-Performance Team?

In his best seller, *Peak Performers: The New Heroes of American Business,* Charles Garfield describes his experience as a novice computer programmer with the Grumman Aerospace team whose assignment was to design and build the Apollo II missions' Lunar Module—the first manned craft to land on the moon:

> Something extraordinary began to happen as the work got under way. Thousands of ordinary men and women who had been competent workers—project managers, secretaries, technicians—suddenly became super-achievers, doing the best work of their lives. Within 18 months, our section moved its performance rating from the bottom 50 percent to the top 15 percent. "Want to know why we're doing so well?" our manager asked me. He pointed to the pale moon barely visible in the eastern sky. "People have been dreaming about going there for thousands of years. And *we're* going to do it."

These individuals came together as a team. They were able to channel their energies toward a common purpose and to accomplish what none of them singly could possibly accomplish. The technical term for this phenomenon is *synergism.*

SYNERGISM AND THE HIGH-PERFORMANCE TEAM

***Synergism* is the simultaneous actions of separate entities which together have greater total effect than the sum of their individual effects.**

In other words, synergism is focusing a group's efforts so that 2 + 2 = 5. Have you ever been part of a high-performance team and experienced this synergism? Take a few minutes and write down some words to describe this experience.

You probably experienced exhilaration, stimulation, satisfaction, a sense of challenge and purpose, a natural high.

Also recall some examples of synergism and high-performance teams in your everyday life, either your personal life or work-related examples.

Athletics provides a multitude of examples, particularly team sports such as basketball, football, soccer, rowing, relay races, hockey, etc. It is not only the individual athletes' abilities, but their work as a team that produces winners.

Other good examples of synergism come from the music world. Recall the power and energy produced by a top-notch marching band or symphony orchestra. It is up to each individual to know his or her part. There may be some solos, but ultimately what is important is how it all sounds together. Is the whole greater than the sum of its parts?

Business, too, abounds with examples of synergism. Bennis and Nanus, in *Leaders* cite the example of a famous city planner and developer, James Rouse:

> When he was dissatisfied with the looks of some housing in his Columbia, Maryland, project, he tried to influence the next design by nagging and correcting his team of architects. He got nowhere. Then he decided to stop "correcting" them and tried to influence them by sending them to look at the world's best, demonstrating what he wanted, what he was for. Inspired by Rouse's vision, the architects went on to create some of the most eye-catching and functional housing in the country.

Or consider what typically happens on a broader scale when starting a new business. One critical function often "champions" the new opportunity: marketing because of a customer, research because of a new idea, or manufacturing because of production capability. True synergism, however, exists when people from all three functions agree on the new business target. Invariably in this case the energy of the team and the pace of commercialization accelerates and the odds of success of the new business venture increase.

The challenge is to create a situation where you and your work unit function as a team to achieve more than each can as individuals. In fact, the real payoff—the most important contribution you can make as a manager—is to produce synergy in your work unit. An important starting point for examining high-performing teams and how to produce synergy is to look at your role as an *energy manager.*

THE ENERGY BUSINESS

If you were on an airplane, seated next to a man wearing a large white cowboy hat, and if, in the course of your conversation, he stated that he was in the energy business, what would you think he did? The obvious answer is something to do with oil. But managers are also in the energy business; that is, people are limited energy resources, and how employees use their energy in the course of an eight to ten hour day is a significant determinant on how they produce and perform.

As a manager, one of your primary responsibilities is to help your employees focus as much human energy on their work as possible.

Kinds of Energy

Your employees bring four different forms of human energy to their jobs: physical, mental, emotional, and energy-of-the-spirit.

- **Physical energy** is the energy expended doing muscular work—walking, standing for long periods, playing games, exercising.
- **Mental energy** is the energy consumed in brain work—reading, writing, talking with people, sitting in conferences and meetings, struggling with problems, planning.
- **Emotional energy** is the energy that helps keep a person's physical and mental machinery in momentum. This form of energy is, to a great extent, responsible for accomplishments from hour to hour and day to day.
- **Energy-of-the-spirit** is the form of energy that might be likened to electricity. When it flows through you, it sparks your spirits, gives you a sense of buoyancy. You are confident and resourceful. You work with decision, enjoy your work, are alive. Energy-of-the-spirit is what allows people to spark one another and creates synergism. This powerful form of energy helps everyone do hard tasks easily, to put spirit into doing the most humdrum jobs, to go through the day with spring in their steps, and to work long hours without weariness.

Understanding and appreciating the limits of the four forms of energy is the first step toward understanding how to help employees direct their energy toward their work. The quality of the work experience depends on the degree to which all four forms of energy are engaged in the work and properly conserved. This book will help you energize the members of your work unit.

Directing Energy

Robert Half, founder and head of the world's largest recruitment network specializing in financial and data processing positions, coined the term "time theft" to describe: "the millions of hours lost each day because of employees who purposely abuse the time they should be spending on the job. Time theft includes excessive socializing, conducting personal business, or doing almost nothing at all." According to a study conducted by Half's organization, theft of time by employees in the United States was approximately $140 billion dollars a year.

Your job as manager is to direct your team members' energies toward productivity. The amount of energy they elect to direct toward work-related activities can be viewed on a continuum, as illustrated in Figure 1.

People who give low energy to the work situation fall on the left side of the scale running from 0 to 100. Employees who give little energy to their jobs, much less than 50 percent, are described as low performers or problem employees—time thieves.

A second group of employees perform at around 40–60 percent of their potential energy and are described as average, marginal, or acceptable workers. This group is often described by managers as "their" group. Some of these employees will never change because their only motivation is to trade time for

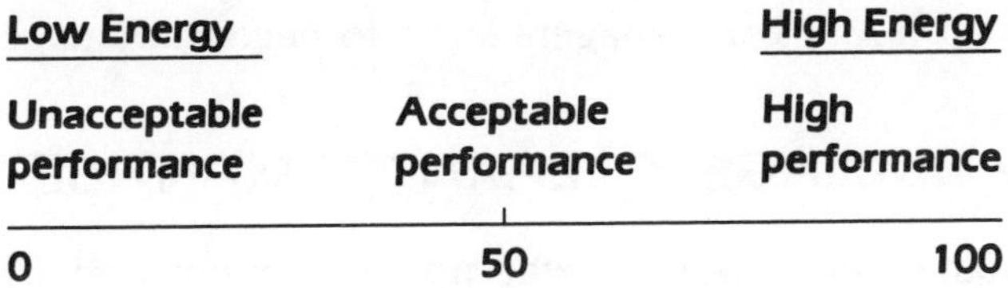

Low Energy		High Energy
Unacceptable performance	Acceptable performance	High performance
0	50	100

Figure 1 Energy continuum.

money. But many of these people have the potential to give more energy to their jobs and to become high performers.

A third group of employees consistently give greater than 60 percent of their energy. Such people are described as high performers, achievers. In fact, high-quality performers can be described as those who give 75–100 percent of their energy in all its forms toward productive work. In addition, the presence of the fourth form of energy, that of the spirit, accounts for those rare occasions described as giving 110 percent.

If one of your roles is to manage people to become high performers, consider how you currently deal with employees at different points along the continuum. How do you, as a manager, currently attempt to get those individuals in the 0–40 percent category to give more energy to their jobs? What about the people giving 40–60 percent? And those over 60 percent? Think of how you spend your time and energy with each group.

For those in the 0–40 percent energy expenditure category, you might typically set very specific goals and tasks, provide frequent follow-up, use reprimands or threats, spend a lot of time coaching, and provide frequent feedback. If these tactics do not work, dismissal is often necessary. For those in the 40–60 percent category, you might typically attempt to catch the employees doing things right and reward them, give them more latitude, and encourage them to improve. You might give those in the top category more responsibility along with more freedom and autonomy. You might also engage in mutual goal setting, and provide bonuses or social rewards.

If you are like most managers, the majority of your efforts to help employees direct more energy toward their jobs involve interacting with each employee one-to-one. This is understandable given how most managers learn to become managers.

HOW MANAGERS LEARN TO MANAGE

Most managers work their way up to their position. They begin as *doers.* The Management vs. Doer Diagram (Figure 2)

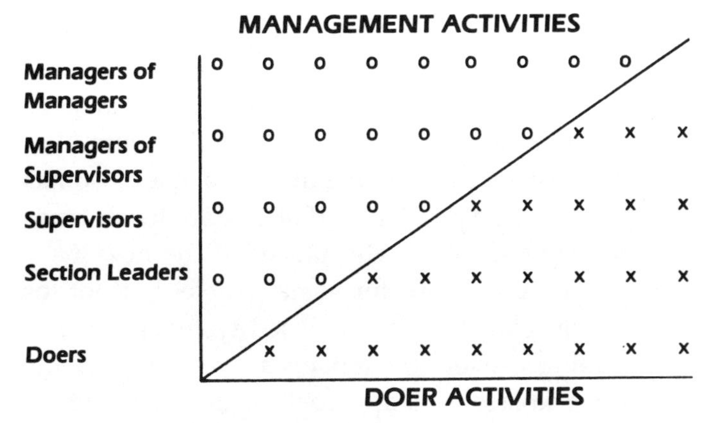

Figure 2 Management vs. doer.

illustrates the typical upward progression of the doers in an organization.

A doer is anyone in a nonsupervisory capacity, as, for example, engineers, clerical workers, sales representatives, assemblers, testers, secretaries. The X's indicate that their day is taken up totally with doer activities. In many cases, people are promoted because they are the best working in their particular function. When they become a section head or supervisor, they begin to take on more management activities, but continue to spend a large part of their time with tasks they used to perform as doers. Why is that so? Consider your own situation; if you came up the ranks as a doer, how did you respond and think?

At the lower levels of management, when the pressure is on to get something done, the tendency is to continue to think and react as a doer and get it done rather than to teach the members of the work unit to do it.

As managers continue to rise in the organization, they find themselves spending more and more time on management activities, represented by O's, and less and less time in doer activities. They usually learn management activities from watching others, from modeling their bosses, or through trial and error.

Advantages in learning to manage this way are that there is consistency of thinking and, if the model is good, the learners learn the right things. In addition, doing as well as managing becomes part of the manager's reward system and is what will likely get further promotions. It also enhances the manager's comfort level knowing that the employees depend on him.

Unfortunately, learning to manage in this manner also has negative consequences. One problem is that this approach tends to perpetuate the way managers who preceded the new managers managed, which may work for some people, but not for others. This approach tends to foster a closed system as well as dependence on doing. Given the changes occurring in the world and in the workplace, this approach to the management issue needs to be reexamined.

While it is understandable that managers who are former doers probably rely on a one-to-one approach, and that this approach *does* have its value, does it accomplish work the most effective, efficient way? Do managers have the time and energy to deal with all employees one-to-one? Does the size of the work unit realistically allow this? Take a few minutes to answer these questions.

MANAGING ONE-TO-ONE VS. ONE-TO-GROUP

The challenge of creating a high-performance team rather than a group of high performing individuals is twofold:

1. To begin to think like higher-level managers without ever forgetting what it is like to be at lower levels, especially in the world of the doers.
2. To begin to think more in terms of one-to-group management.

The importance of accepting this challenge is illustrated in the following scenario.

Russ Stewart, head of the design division of a manufacturing operation, is seated in his office talking on the telephone. He hangs up the phone, sighs, hurriedly finishes writing a lengthy list of things to do, gathers up an armful of rolled design plans, and rushes out of his office. As he flies down the hall, he brushes past one of his team members, making no acknowledgment as Frank flattens himself against the wall to let his busy manager past.

Russ charges into Andrea's office, startling her. He brusquely informs her that he's just gotten the go-ahead for the Carrington project, a project which had been on hold. She's to drop whatever she's working on and focus on Carrington. Andrea protests that she's in the middle of another high priority project, but Russ insists Carrington is more important and strides briskly out of her office, down the hall, and into Bud's office.

He relays the same message to Bud and receives essentially the same protestations. As he had done with Andrea, Russ insists that Bud put his current project on hold in deference to the Carrington project, hands him the new specs, and departs, leaving a bewildered Bud staring at the specs.

Glancing at his watch, Russ sees it's almost time for a budget meeting he isn't quite prepared for and quickens his pace even more. As he approaches his office, he encounters another member of his team and informs him about the new priority. He hands Jerry the new specifications for his area of responsibility and tells him that if he has any questions, he'll be back in his office at around 3:00.

Russ hurriedly returns to his desk and is working on his budget figures when Bud appears in his doorway with a question about the project he had been working on. Russ is incredulous. He informs Bud that he's not to even be thinking about any project other than Carrington, at which point his phone rings. He answers it and signals for Bud to leave.

While Russ is in his budget meeting, the members of his team gather together and complain to one another about the shift in priorities. They have numerous questions that none of them can answer. All decide they will go to see Russ as soon as he gets out of his meeting.

Russ probably believes he is getting the project started, communicating with his people, giving out assignments, delegating authority, and establishing deadlines—all appropriate management activities. If you've been in a similar management situation, you can understand his feelings of being hassled, rushed, and stressed. In fact, however, Russ's energy was spent doing things one-to-one—not an efficient use of energy.

Reverse perspectives for a moment. Most members of the work unit probably thought the manager was miscommunicating, not supplying needed information, creating confusion, and causing stress. They probably felt frustrated, confused, and angry. In such a case, they are likely to spend their energy complaining, to seek further clarification, and to want more time with management.

Imagine a different scenario. It is a replay of Russ Stewart in his office on the telephone.

> This time, after hanging up the phone and finishing his list of things to do, rather than rushing off to talk to the members of his team individually, Russ buzzes his secretary and asks her to call the Carrington project team together for a meeting. At this meeting Russ explains that the Carrington project has the go-ahead and must take precedence over *all* other projects. He lets them voice their objections and tells them he understands how frustrating it can be to have to drop something when you're right in the middle. He points out that the faster they get Carrington finished, the sooner they can return to their other projects.
>
> Russ then distributes the specifications for the individual areas to the responsible team members and goes over them one by one. Midway through the discussion Andrea points out that any changes Jerry makes in the input module could affect how all the components fit. Other instances of overlap are identified, and the need to work together is stressed. Russ then sets the next meeting, encouraging them to keep each other and him informed about their progress and any problems that arise between this meeting and the next. As he leaves to attend his budget meeting, the team members are enthusiastically discussing where to begin work on the changes required in the Carrington project.

In the second scenario, the manager's energy was spent getting the team together, promoting cross-communication, and facilitating the project start-up. Members of the work unit spent their energy getting involved, looking for ways to make the project work, expressing willingness to trade assignments, and getting each other "pumped up."

The two scenarios reflect two management strategies applied to the same situation. In the first, the manager interacts one-to-one with members of the work unit. One-to-one skills are essential to good management, but in certain situations these skills are inefficient because of the time and energy it takes for the number of employees involved. The second strategy—one-to-group—can be more effective and efficient, creating a situation where people perform at higher levels.

The purpose of this book is to expand your skill base to include one-to-group skills, skills designed to help you as a manager assist your work unit in becoming a high-performing team.

In short, this book presents a philosophy of management that takes into consideration the ideas of employee involvement, but goes beyond the traditional ideas of quality circles, task forces, or team building. It recognizes the importance of one-to-one skills. It is not an either/or situation. It is having the skills to use both approaches, depending on the situation. In fact, when using the one-to-group approach, it is important to remember that this approach is not a panacea for all management problems.

THE ZONE OF INSPIRATION

You can expect the one-to-group management approach to result in higher performance from your people. The reason for these improved results is depicted in Figure 3, a model illustrating goal setting, risk, and performance.

This diagram portrays what people experience as they commit to pursuing goals at various levels of risk. If they set

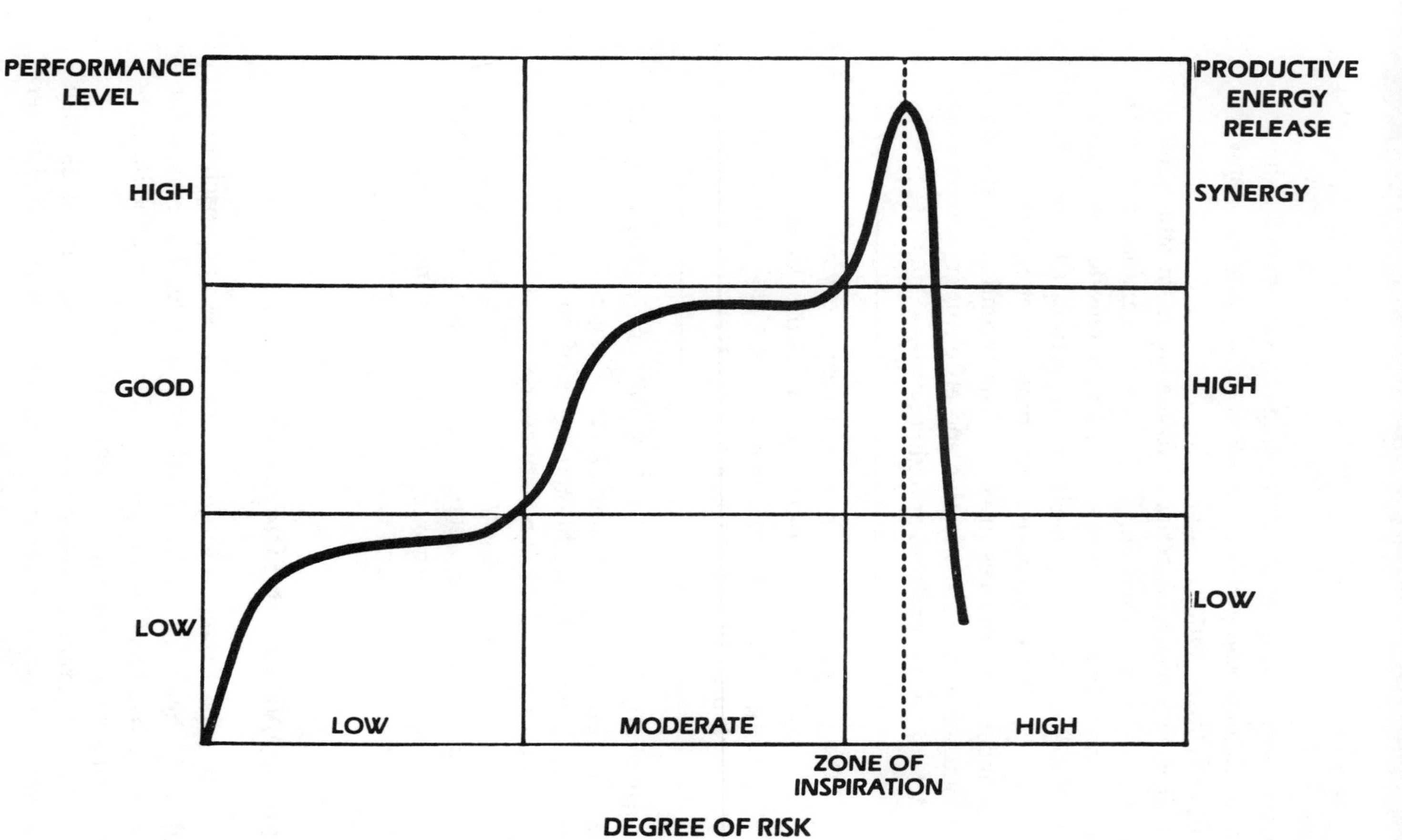

Figure 3 Achieving synergy.

their goals low (in relation to their true capability), not much of their productive energy is engaged. What they achieve is well below their potential. At this level there is not much risk of failure, but also not much satisfaction in what is achieved.

Moving into the zone of moderate risk, where the chances of success are roughly 50/50 allows for much more of their productive energy to be released. The level of performance rises as well as their satisfaction. If goals are set too high—where the chances of success are very small—productive energy tends to be wasted and they commonly experience failure as well as frustration.

On some occasions, however, everything seems to come together for people. They find themselves pursuing a goal that is near the boundary between moderate risk and high risk. This narrow zone is the *zone of inspiration.* In this zone people perform as if they were experiencing greater energy than they were supplying by themselves—synergism. According to Bennis and Nanus:

> Consultants often report that they can feel this energy almost from the first moment they enter a corporation. It was present at Polaroid when Edwin Land led that firm into a new age of photography and at Sears, Roebuck and Co. when the decision was made to become a financial services powerhouse. It takes the form of enthusiasm, commitment, pride, willingness to work hard and "go the extra mile."

Recall the earlier example of the importance of "champions" in each critical function necessary to accomplish a goal. Those champions, when committing to complete each important task, normally arrive at a consensus of the expected outcome. This consensus team view will help inspire the champions at the time when their individual tasks become frustrating and their productive energy begins to decrease.

EIGHT ATTRIBUTES OF THE HIGH-PERFORMING TEAM

Wilson research has identified eight attributes typically present in teams that perform in the zone of inspiration:

- **Participative leadership**—creating an interdependency by empowering, freeing up, and serving others
- **Shared responsibility**—establishing an environment in which all team members feel as responsible as the manager for the performance of the work unit
- **Aligned on purpose**—having a sense of common purpose about why the team exists and the function it serves
- **High communication**—creating a climate of trust and open, honest communication
- **Future focused**—seeing change as an opportunity for growth
- **Focused on task**—keeping meetings focused on results
- **Creative talents**—applying individual talents and creativity
- **Rapid response**—identifying and acting on opportunities

You may be thinking: this is common sense. And that's the good news. As Thomas Edison astutely observed: "Common sense is genius in its working clothes." You already know how important these eight attributes are, but are you using them or simply paying lip service to them as you manage your work unit? The rest of this book will take you step by step through each attribute, help you assess whether it is present in your work unit, and, if it is not present, offer suggestions about how you can go about developing it.

An important aspect of how you apply the specific attributes is to consider how teams develop. They don't happen overnight, but rather go through developmental stages.

THREE PHASES OF TEAM DEVELOPMENT

Establishing a high-performance team is a developmental process. That is, a work unit must go through several phases of growth and change to become a high-performance team. Most work units go through three phases, but all groups are not alike. Each passes through the phases at different rates and exhibits different patterns of interactions at each phase. Some indicators of team development, however, transcend these differences. You, as a manager, should consider these indicators, illustrated in Figure 4, as you assess your team's development.

Phase 1: Collection of Individuals. When people are asked to work together, they initially form a collection of *individuals.* This first phase gives individuals the opportunity to form identities within the work unit. Phase 1 teams tend to be individual-centered, have individual goals rather than group goals, do not share responsibility, avoid changes, and do not deal with conflict. Members begin to define their purpose and responsibilities, identify the skills of other members, and develop norms for working with one another.

Phase 2: Groups. In the second developmental phase, work units begin forming *groups.* Members develop a group identity, define their roles, clarify their purpose, and establish norms for working together. However, groups tend to be leader-centered; the leader provides direction, assigns tasks, reviews performance, and is the primary focus of communication.

Phase 3: Team. The final phase, and difficult to attain, is that of an actual high-performance team, a team able to focus energy, respond rapidly to opportunities, and share both responsibilities and rewards. Teams are purpose-centered; members not only understand the purpose but are committed to it and use the purpose to guide actions and decisions.

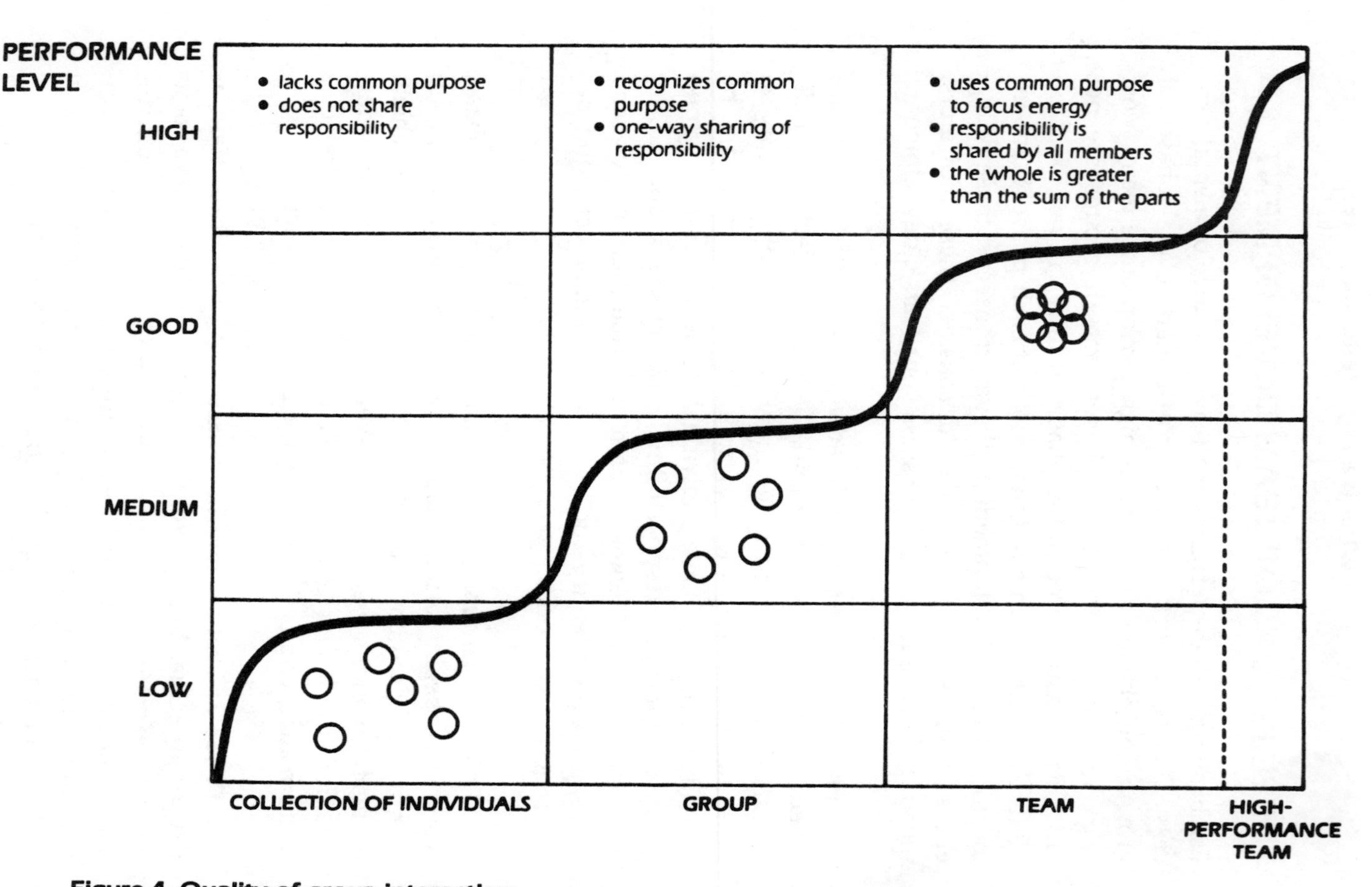

Figure 4 Quality of group interaction.

Work units differ in a number of ways, and a variety of factors contribute to any one work unit's development as a team. Some units have not been interacting for a long time or have experienced change or reorganization. New units will probably be in the early phases of development. Units that have been together for longer periods may also be in early phases of team development, but for other reasons. Some tasks do not require Phase 3 interaction, and therefore a group will not exhibit these characteristics. And some work units have not developed the skills necessary for interacting at the Phase 3 level.

One of your tasks as a manager is to identify those attributes currently helping your team to high performance and those preventing it. The rest of this book will help you do so.

The final test of a leader is that he leaves behind him in other men the conviction and the will to carry on.
—Walter Lippman, on the death of Roosevelt.

Do what I say, not what I do.

2

Participative Leadership: The Changing Role of Managers

Ask Yourself . . .

- Do you assign individual tasks and methods?
- Do your employees follow rules and comply with your requests?
- Do you direct and monitor your employees' progress on tasks?
- Do you set an appropriate example for your work team?

Fran Tarkenton, holder of numerous records for his skill as a quarterback, was a player/coach, usually calling his own plays and sparking the team to work together. He sometimes let his linemen suggest plays because they were closer to the action than he or the headcoach. It was not only his ability to throw the ball or to scramble that put him into the Football Hall of Fame; it was his ability to coach and lead on the field.

In a high-performing team, the manager is one of the members, participating with the rest of the employees. This is not to imply that the work unit functions like a democracy or that the manager is not responsible for what does or does not happen, in the work unit. It suggests, however, that you may get better results by leading rather than managing in the traditional sense of the word.

LEADERSHIP

An advertisement in *The Wall Street Journal* says: "People don't want to be managed, they want to be lead." It notes that we do not talk about world managers, but rather about world leaders.

One relevant description of leadership was written in the Sixth Century BC by Lao-Tzu:

> The superior leader gets things done
> With very little motion.
> He imparts instruction not through many words
> But through a few deeds.
> He keeps informed about everything
> But interferes hardly at all.
> He is a catalyst,
> And although things wouldn't get done as well
> If he weren't there,
> When they succeed he takes no credit.
> And because he takes no credit
> Credit never leaves him.

John H. Zenger in *Leadership: Management's Better Half* provides another definition of leadership: "Leaders . . . provide visionary inspiration, motivation and direction. Leadership generates an emotional connection between the leader and the led. Leadership attracts people and inspires them to put forth incredible efforts in a common cause." Zenger cautions, however, that: "All leadership and no management would be as serious a problem as our current imbalance in the other direction."

A parallel can be found in the educational world and the difference in teaching approaches. According to William Arthur Ward: "The mediocre teacher tells, the good teacher explains, the superior teacher demonstrates, and the great teacher inspires." There's quite a span from simply telling to inspiring. You can probably think of teachers who fit into each of these categories. And those who did inspire you probably did so because they made you make the most of your abilities; they helped you to grow. The same opportunity is available to you as a manager.

An important mandate for managers is helping employees grow.

In fact, one issue that surfaces whenever employees are surveyed regarding what they expect from their work experience is *the chance to grow.* Too often the focus is on getting results; but people need to feel good about themselves and what they're doing. It should come as no surprise that managers who are perceived as having the most positive influence are those managers who help their employees grow in their approach toward their work.

STAGES OF GROWTH

One important aspect of this maturing is the way employees relate to their manager and to each other. The typical stages of growth are illustrated in Figure 1.

The first stage of growth is referred to as the *dependent* stage. At the dependent stage, employees are just learning the job and are very dependent on the direction of others. The

	GROWTH 1	2	3
Employee Growth Stage	Dependent	Independent	Interdependent
Management Role	Tell	Influence	Collaborate
Human Analogy	Child	Adolescent	Adult

Figure 1 The stages of growth.

relationship is much like that between a child and a parent. Employees at this stage of growth are often described as searching, watching, following, needing direction. Your role as manager of a person at this stage is to use a *tell* approach: to give specific directions; to set small, more immediate goals; and to give frequent feedback, both positive and negative. The tell approach is usually appropriate at this level because the employees need direction and support as they learn a new job or task. With the proper direction, you may help your employees begin to grow and develop.

As employees grow and develop, they become more *independent.* At the independent stage, employees begin to perform on their own. They master the performance by repeating the same processes and methods over and over. This relationship resembles that between a parent and an adolescent. Employees at this stage of growth can be described as maintaining, being responsible, contributing, desiring independence. They no longer depend on you for knowledge and skills, but they need to be influenced regarding the use of their energy and level of expected performance.

If you, as manager, remain in the tell mode with employees who are becoming independent and responsible, you create a compliance environment where people give you *time* because that's what they are being paid for, but they don't give you energy. Such employees may become resentful if they are not allowed more freedom.

At this stage in employees' growth, you should give them more responsibility, more freedom, ask for input and suggestions, engage in mutual goal setting, and make feedback more of a two-way communication. Most managers who can bring their employees along to this stage, to get them up to speed and independent feel they have done their job, that it is the traditional role of management to move people from dependence to independence. The key to participative leadership takes it one step further.

Creating the high-performance team requires you to go one step beyond—moving people to being *interdependent*.

The role of the manager shifts to that of a collaborator—similar to the relationship of a parent to an adult offspring. An employee at this stage of growth can be described as cooperating, caring for, assisting, supporting, and uniting.

Interdependence is a way to relate to each other that recognizes and uses each member's strengths to connect so as to minimize the effect of each member's weaknesses.

At this stage, your role as manager is to help/mentor employees, solicit feedback from them, establish parameters, allow input on how to accomplish the tasks at hand, and give more responsibility. Often managers who are asked if they could change only one behavior in their boss that would have the greatest impact on human energy answer that they would ask for a boss who would ask more and tell less.

A unique benefit of creating interdependence is the sense of community that develops between members of the work unit. This creates an atmosphere that is not only productive, but also humanly satisfying. Equally important, it also contributes to a high degree of synergy, with the group collectively accomplishing more than each member could working independently. By creating interdependence, the group shares the responsibility for what is occurring in the work unit.

Leadership is critical in getting employees past the independent stage and to the interdependent stage. To do so, managers must rethink the traditional way of managing.

AUTHORITATIVE VS. PARTICIPATIVE LEADERSHIP

You probably learned to be a manager using the authoritative approach: telling employees what to do until they finally were able to do it without being told—dependent to independent. Wilson Learning research shows that moving employees toward interdependence requires that the manager shift toward the *participative* approach, as illustrated in Figure 2.

SPECTRUM OF LEADER BEHAVIOR

Authoritative ———————————————— Participative

Figure 2 Spectrum of leader behavior.

It is easier to be autocratic and tell people what to do, but this approach does not build a high-performance team. It fosters dependence rather than interdependence. The model in Figure 3 shows the differences between the two approaches.

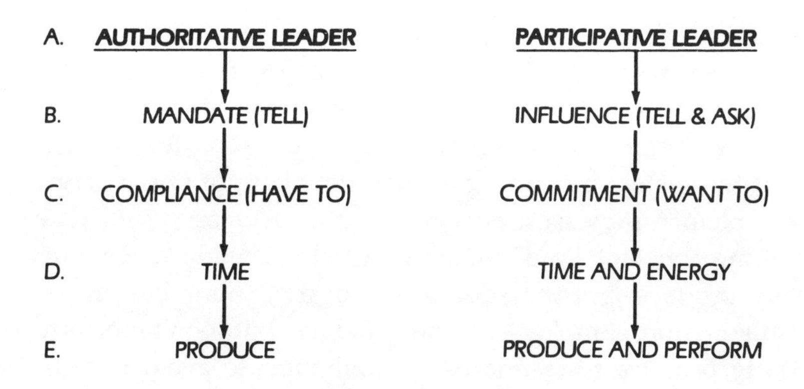

- Communication is downward; little upward communication
- Position power
- Tell oriented
- People do things because they "have to"
- People put in their time
- Energy decreases
- People produce to standard

- Greater upward and lateral communication
- Personal power
- Tell and ask oriented
- People do things because they "want to"
- People put in their time **and** their energy
- People perform more than "just the expected"

Figure 3 Authoritative vs. participative leader.

As you think about the preceding model, remember, it is not usually an either-or-choice. At times the authoritative approach is needed, as when you get a new employee or if the fire alarm goes off, you smell smoke, and you have not conducted a fire drill. This is not the time for creative brainstorming on the best way to evacuate. Keeping that in mind, compare what usually occurs with these two varying leadership styles.

First, in an authority-based system, most communication is downward in the form of a mandate. It is tell-oriented communication that is typically worded: "you will . . . ." "policy is set that . . ." Such a tell-oriented system usually results in compliance, employees doing things because they have to, and not because they want to. Employees soon learn to get back at the system by putting in their time but not their energy. As compliance increases, energy tends to decrease, with time remaining constant. And finally, in a tell-oriented system, employees produce, but they do not perform, a subtle but important distinction. Employees who produce but don't perform typically produce to standards or minimums to avoid punishment. They have little interest in quality, change, or opportunity. It is from such employees you are likely to hear, "That's not my job." Employees do what they're told and no more. The atmosphere is like a hive of drone bees, busy but mindless. A further disadvantage of such an approach to employees is that it doesn't build second tier management.

How would a participative approach differ? What would the work unit be like? Picture the following scenario:

> The manager of the work unit, Melonie, has called her team together to discuss their upcoming presentation to the management committee. She begins by discussing the agenda for the meeting and asks if anyone wants to add anything to the schedule.
>
> Stan replies that he would like an overview of how Melonie sees the presentation. Melonie tells Stan that's a good idea and adds an update to the agenda. With the agenda settled, Melonie moves on to discuss assignments for the presentation. She explains that she has made the assignments based on what she feels are their areas of strength, but she recognizes there may be other factors like schedules or other assignments that may need to be considered.
>
> At this point Fred raises a question about the software analysis reports, the assignment of his group. He feels Stan's people have been closer to the software analysis than his group, and Stan concurs. Stan suggests they could switch if Fred could take the internal budgeting report. His people are familiar with that.

Fred, however, isn't too receptive to the suggestion, fearing it may be more than his team can handle. Melonie asks Fred to look at the internal budgeting report and see if he could make a switch with Stan. She explains that she can't load down Stan's people with both the software analysis and internal budgeting.

Fred accepts this suggestion and agrees to talk with Stan about it after the meeting.

Harold interjects that he has some data that may be helpful in the software analysis and offers it to Stan.

Linda, who has been attentive, but quiet to this point in the meeting, says she could use some help meeting the schedule; she's swamped. Melonie asks if anyone has some time they could volunteer to help Linda out.

Harold offers to help, indicating he doesn't have a lot of time, but he is good at organizing things, and they arrange a meeting for Friday.

Melonie asks if there are any other questions about the schedule. When none is forthcoming, she sets their next meeting for the following Thursday at 11:00. General consensus are voiced. Melonie ends the meeting by stating, "Before you go, I want to say how much I appreciate your cooperation and willingness to work together. Thanks."

The participatory style of management provides much greater opportunity for upward communication and for horizontal communication. It is not restricted to downward communication as in authoritative management.

In the participatory style of management, managers base requests for action on more than a position of authority. Their power is personal power rather than position power. *Personal power* is that which you possess because of your own knowledge, skill, and the strength of your own people skills, in contrast to *position power,* that which has been conferred on you by higher authorities.

Position power comes from having created opportunity for upward and lateral communication as well as using influence (rather than position power) to affect change.

MANAGING THROUGH INFLUENCE

The importance of influence management rests on the premise that people do things for their own reasons, not yours.

Cervantes astutely observed: "I can tell where my own shoe pinches me." Your team members have needs you can help them meet. James MacGregor Burns, in *Leadership* contends that: "Most important by far, leaders address themselves to followers' wants, needs and other motivations, as well as to their own, and thus they serve as an independent force in changing the makeup of the followers' motive base through gratifying their motives." Burns calls such leadership *transforming leadership* and gives as the best modern example Gandhi who Burns says "roused and elevated the hopes and demands of millions of Indians and whose life and personality were enhanced in the process." He notes that: "Transcending leadership is dynamic leadership in the sense that the leaders throw themselves into a relationship with followers who will feel 'elevated' by it and often become more active themselves, thereby creating new cadres of leaders."

Using your influence instead of your position power or mandating ability increases the likelihood of your employees getting *committed* to what they are doing. In essence, people do things because they want to, not just because they have to. Put another way, people behave in ways that make sense to them. As commitment increases, employees still give you time, but they also begin to give you their *energy*. They continue to produce (to do what they are told), and they also *perform* (do more than they have to).

Performance is stimulated by the employees' satisfaction with your commitment to high communication and involvement. In short, to create and manage a high-performance team, the participative leadership approach works best, with two-way communication becoming dominant, and influencement management being used to secure commitment.

MANAGING THROUGH EXAMPLE

Effective leaders also model the behaviors they wish to encourage in their team members. Lee Iacocca worked long hours and cut his own salary to $1 a year during Chrysler's financial crisis. Richard Knowlton, president of Hormel at the time they were struggling through a year-long strike, refused to accept the raises offered him by the Board of Directors.

Contrast this with an insurance executive whose company faced a financial crisis and was experiencing layoffs and budget cuts. After the executive called together his team and explained the kinds of cutbacks he expected them to accomplish, he flew by the company's private jet to Pebble Beach for a weekend of golf. Understandably, his team members ignored his pleas for frugality.

WHY DO LEADERS WANT TO BECOME LEADERS?

Participatory leadership may fly in the face of everything you've ever learned or believed about leadership. When people are asked why they think leaders want to be leaders, certain responses come up time and again:

For the glory	For the power
To get respect	To get recognized
For the prestige	To take control
As a duty	For self-fulfillment
For the challenge	For the money

These responses can be summarized under three categories:

- To get *POWER*
- To take *CONTROL*
- To be *SERVED* (get money, respect, recognition, prestige, etc.)

Think for a moment if this fits with your own beliefs about why leaders want to be leaders. Next think for a moment about the characteristics of people who have acted as your leaders. Think of a person who has been an influential leader to you personally, for example, a parent, teacher, coach, boss. When people are asked to do this, they come up with some very interesting characteristics:

Had my best interests in mind	Kept my spirits up
Challenged me	Kept me on track
Helped me over the rough spots	Knew what he or she was doing
Was committed to a goal	Had confidence in me
Was open and caring	Was supportive
Stretched me	Gave me time
Knew my unique abilities	Liked himself or herself and me

These characteristics are quite different from the reasons most people give for why leaders wanted to be leaders.

In most instances, leaders ultimately get power, control, and are served by doing just the *opposite*.

Effective leaders tend to *empower* their people, to *free* them up, and to *serve* them.

Power	**Empower**
Control	**Free up**
Be served	**Serve**

Managing one-to-group focuses on empowering, freeing up, and serving. Empowering suggests that you give responsibility, communicate the importance of each team member, provide the opportunity for value, and allow each participant to become an equal member of the team. Freeing up means you use your people's talents, ideas, insights, and creative/problem-solving abilities. Serving suggests you place yourself in the role of helping to contribute to the growth of others; it is a type of people-oriented *quiet power.* When managers empower, free up, and serve, the work unit gives them power, control, and recognition as a leader.

Bennis and Nanus suggest that:

> . . . leadership is not so much the exercise of power itself as the empowerment of others. Leaders are able to translate intentions into reality by aligning the energies of the organization behind an attractive goal. . . . These leaders lead by pulling rather than by pushing, by inspiring rather than ordering; by creating achievable, though challenging, expectations and rewarding progress toward them rather than by manipulating; by enabling people to use their own initiative and experiences rather than by denying or constraining their experiences and actions.

McGinnis, in *Bringing Out the Best in People,* says:

> The ultimate leaders develop followers who will surpass them. Runners will become coaches and train other athletes who will break their records. Executives will motivate subordinates so successfully that they will become their superiors. And parents, in their devotion to a child, will pull him or her up beside them—and then encourage the child to go even higher.

He cites as an example the daughter of Harry and Ada Mae Day. The Days lived in a four-room adobe house that had no running water, no electricity, and no school within driving distance. When Harry's father died, Harry had to take over his ranch rather than going to Stanford, but he dreamed that one day his daughter would go there. Ada Mae taught the children at home using newspapers, magazines, and books. One summer they took their children to all the state capitals west of the Mississippi River. Years later their daughter did attend Stanford, law school, and went on to become the first woman justice on the U.S. Supreme Court. McGinnis suggests that much of the credit for Sandra Day O'Connor's success "goes to a determined ranch mother sitting in her adobe house, reading to her children by the hour and who, with her husband, scampered up the stairways of capitol domes, their children in tow."

Before leaving the topic of participatory leadership, it is important that you think about your *orientation* to leadership. You can probably list the behaviors and characteristics of effective leaders, but many different styles can be effective. What is important is that you be seen as attempting to empower, free up, and serve others, although the specific behaviors you exhibit may be different from those other managers exhibit. If people believe and trust that your *intent* is to help them grow by empowering them, they will be more forgiving when you behave in ways that may not be as productive as possible. However, if they don't trust your intent, and you suddenly change certain behaviors to be a participative leader, they may not believe you, or they may wonder what you are up to.

The next chapter will look at empowering from the team members' perspective and how it can enable them to share responsibility for the team's accomplishments.

THE PARTICIPATIVE LEADER IN ACTION

Before going on to the next chapter, take a few minutes to consider the attribute of participative leadership and its characteristics in the high-performance team. Locate (Figure 4) where you think you and your work unit are, and if it falls short of the team level, consider the possible actions suggested that might make sense for your work unit.

Teams who score low in this area follow rules and comply with demands. They rely on the leader to assign individual

Phase	Characteristics	Possible Actions
Team: (81 to 100)	• Members help choose tasks, methods, and standards. • Members review process and results. • Members are committed to high performance.	• Encourage group decision-making and consensus. • Reinforce constructive assessment of other group members. • Reinforce commitment and quality results.
Group: (61 to 80)	• Leader assigns tasks with group input. • Leader monitors and evaluates results. • Leader determines standards for performance.	• Allow members to take initiative in choosing tasks. • Encourage self and peer review of performance. • Seek group input on standards for performance and evaluation.
Collection: (0 to 60)	• Leader assigns individual tasks and methods. • Leader directs and monitors progress on tasks. • Members follow rules and comply with demands.	• Seek input before assigning tasks and allow members some discretion in how they accomplish a task. • Support progress and monitor results. • Provide clear standards for performance.

Figure 4 Participative leadership—being committed to high performance.

tasks, indicate how the tasks are to be accomplished, and to direct and monitor their progress.

Teams who score average on participative leadership have their standards for performance predetermined by their leader who also assigns tasks, with some group input, and who monitors and evaluates the results.

Teams who score high on this attribute commit themselves to high performance; they help choose tasks, how to approach them, and how to evaluate them; and they review their own progress and results.

We're all in this together. If we succeed, we all succeed. If we fail, we all fail.

It's not my job, man.

3

Shared Responsibility: Whose Job Is It?

Ask Yourself . . .

- What are you, as manager, responsible for in your work unit?
- Do your employees benefit from individual contributions to the group?
- Do people feel like stakeholders of the business?
- Do employees help each other acquire new skills?
- Are individual roles clearly understood by all employees?
- Does everyone feel responsible for the success or failure of a meeting or for the unit's goals?

In a Southern California thermodynamics plant, a unit of technicians whose routine, repetitive task was to check temperatures and pressures on the plant's delicate equipment, consistently achieved an outstanding performance record and also the lowest turnover rate in the company. The foreman pointed out that each employee wore a green surgical smock, gifts from his son, a cardiovascular surgeon. He impressed upon his team that they were to take care of the plant's delicate equipment just like a doctor takes care of human hearts and that as long as their team was working, there wouldn't be any failures. The employees, only half jokingly, call each other "Doctor." This group spirit, this sense of being part of something worthwhile, makes them into a high-performance team.

THE TRADITIONAL VIEW

As you examine your role as a manager and understand the need for more participative leadership, you also need to address the issue of responsibility, including responsibility for what happens in a work unit. The traditional view is that managers alone are responsible for what occurs in the work unit. Recall Harry S. Truman's famous, "The buck stops here."

But is this view practical? Is it only *your* tail that's on the line? Can you afford to be the *heroic manager,* carrying the entire work unit on your back? Do you want to?

Bradford and Cohen, in *Managing for Excellence,* describe the *heroic manager,* as one who tries to have all the answers, who accepts responsibility for performance of the work unit, who feels he or she must be in control, must coordinate and direct all efforts. When a problem arises, that manager is like the Lone Ranger rushing to the rescue, leaving only a silver bullet upon his departure.

Unfortunately, such heroism does not teach people to fend for themselves. In fact, it sets into motion a vicious circle that is self-fulfilling, self-perpetuating, and self-reinforcing, with team members becoming more passive and accepting less responsibility, and the heroic manager being forced to take on more responsibility.

Bradford and Cohen argue there are several reasons to believe the heroic style of management is outdated. The reasons are closely tied to changes occurring in the workplace. It has changed from simple to complex, requiring more reliance on technology and experts in specific areas. It has changed from reliance upon independence to reliance upon interdependence. The early 1900s emphasis on specialization has been replaced with an emphasis on teams of experts working toward a common goal. Even change itself has changed, with the pace accelerating year by year.

AN ALTERNATIVE VIEW

These changes have led to the need for a *post-heroic leader,* one who creates an environment where team members share responsibility for managing the unit *with* the manager. All are committed to the success of the department. This requires a shift in mindset to the manager as developer, building a shared responsibility team by making key departmental decisions jointly with team members, and helping team members feel jointly responsible for department successes and failures. It involves identifying and gaining commitment to a tangible *vision*—a unique, challenging, important, exciting task to accomplish. It also means providing for continuous individual development. Each of the preceding is discussed in depth in later chapters.

The differences between heroic management and post-heroic leadership can be summarized as follows:

1. The heroic manager feels personally responsible for the success of the department; the post-heroic leader helps members increase their sense of responsibility of managing the department.
2. The heroic manager tries personally to figure out solutions to problems and sell them to subordinates; the post-heroic leader facilitates the subordinates to be more skilled in and committed to solving core department problems.
3. The heroic manager tries personally to control what goes on; the post-heroic leader builds control into the

system by facilitating peers in feeling responsible for control and coordination.

4. The heroic manager finds satisfaction in solving touchy problems; the post-heroic leader finds satisfaction in seeing individuals and the team succeeding and developing as a high-performing department.

The job of the post-heroic leader is to create the conditions in which members share in the responsibility of managing the department, work together to solve core departmental problems, and share in the responsibility of insuring sufficient control and coordination.

THE MANAGER'S DILEMMA

Cohen and Bradford suggest that many managers are trapped in the "Superman vs. Clark Kent Syndrome"; that is, they either over control, flying to the rescue, or they undercontrol, showing no semblance of strength. Even worse, they may vacillate between the two and "spend their life in the phone booth." They note that the manager's dilemma is to provide a challenging task with autonomy and *still* insure sufficient coordination and control. They liken it to a wagon master with a team of horses facing the challenge of getting all the horses pulling together without tightening the reins so much the horses rebel or dropping the reins so they run wild.

THE IMPORTANCE OF RESPONSIBILITY

Have you ever been in a situation where you felt absolutely no responsibility, perhaps even had none? Maybe you have attended a seminar where the presentor was bombing? Played on a team consisting of all stars? Attended a meeting with no agenda and everyone was free wheeling it? Or been part of a work unit expected simply to obey orders from the top? Think about how it felt. You probably felt limited, frustrated, or maybe simply disinterested. What was your energy level? Can you recall how others in the group reacted? Most likely they exhibited low excitement, apathy, lack of concern for anyone other than themselves. And imagine how the person in charge—the presentor, coach, meeting leader, work unit manager—must have felt. Probably stressed, frustrated, and inefficient, yet totally responsible for the situation.

Perpetuating the Traditional View

What is it that managers do to perpetuate the myth that the manager has sole responsibility? Several actions can foster this notion: restricting opportunities for employees to talk to each other on the job, insisting that all questions be directed to them, withholding information from members of the group, giving out only small pieces of a task or not telling employees what the whole task is, insisting on having everything go through the manager, not cross-training employees. There are probably others you can think of. The result is something like the situation depicted in this brief but pointed little story:

> Once upon a time there was a work unit with four members named Everybody, Somebody, Anybody, and Nobody. There was an important job to be done, and Everybody was sure that Somebody would do it. Anybody could have done it, but Nobody did it. Somebody got angry about that because it was Everybody's job. Everybody thought Anybody could do it, but Nobody realized that Everybody wouldn't do it. It ended up that Everybody blamed Somebody when Nobody did what Anybody could have done.

TEAMWORK

True teamwork occurs in situations where members are performance-dependent on each other. It is not simply a togetherness. Members of a basketball team, for example, depend on each other on each play. They pass the ball back and forth, and the actions of one player influence the actions of all the others. This is in contrast to individuals on a bowling team. Each bowler's score results from only that bowler's actions; it is not influenced by what other individuals on the team do.

To create a high-performance team, it is important that the work to be performed does rely on teamwork rather than on isolated, individual efforts.

In high-performance teams, members pull together, help each other out, recognize and complement each other's strengths and weaknesses, and share a belief that they are responsible to each other.

It is one important result of participative leadership, discussed in Chapter 2. Bennis and Nanus's *Leaders* (p. 80) says that the effect of this type of leadership on the work force is that such leaders:

> *empower others to translate intention into reality and sustain it.* This does not mean that leaders must relinquish power, or that followers must continually challenge authority. It does mean that power must become a unit of exchange—an active, changing token in creative, productive, and communicative transactions. Effective leaders will ultimately reap the human harvest of their efforts by the simple action of power's reciprocal: *empowerment.* It puts the duality in motion—power to empowerment, empowerment back to power. Almost the way conductor and players or leaders and subordinates play off one another, building into a crescendo of harmonious voices, an epiphany of human effort. This reciprocity creates its own rhythm, its own vitality and momentum.

Henry Ford could, and did, know everything about the Ford; he wasn't forced to rely upon his work units. In contrast, Lee Iacocca couldn't possibly know everything about the various Chrysler lines. Yet Iacocca stands as a stellar example of a manager who could lead a workforce from failure to success.

He was able to create a high-performance team by sharing responsibility.

Today managers, faced with rapid technological changes, masses of information available at the press of a button, and changing values in the workforce, are becoming more and more convinced that they should and must share responsibility if they are to accomplish their goals. And with shared responsibility, both managers and employees benefit greatly.

Recall the stages of growth from childhood to adolescence to adulthood and the parallel between the individual employee, the group of employees, and the team—the growth from *dependence* to *independence* to *interdependence.* Do parents who really care for their children shoulder all responsibility for them, encourage them to remain single, live at home, to be taken care of as long as they follow the parents' rules? Highly unlikely. The parallel between managers and employees is not difficult to envision. Yet many managers thrive on the belief that their work unit can't get along without them; they are indispensable. In reality, the opposite is usually true. The manager whose work unit functions smoothly without the manager's being there has achieved what should be striven for: a work unit where people work together to accomplish something they perceive to be important, because they want to, not because the manager is there with a stick.

Picture yourself as a participant in the following scenario:

> Melonie's group is in a meeting engaged in lively conversation. She is explaining to them that if they're going to meet the new deadline, it is critical for each of them to be aware of how everyone else is doing on their assignments. Fred emphatically agrees that the need for keeping each other informed is becoming more and more apparent. Stan chimes in that at least they are all in it together.
>
> Melonie reminds them that helping each other is the only way they are going to meet the deadline. If one of them misses a deadline, they all miss it. That means they will have to keep in touch with one another more often than they are used to. The meeting adjourns with the team members eager to dig in.

Two weeks later, the deadline is met, and Melonie calls the group together and praises them, saying, "I didn't know if we could do it, but you really pulled together on this one. You not only met the deadline, but everyone is impressed with the quality of your product. Great job."

Think for a few minutes about how the manager encouraged members of the work unit to share responsibility.

You probably noticed that the manager made it clear that meeting the deadline would require that they help each other as well as the consequences to the whole work unit if one of them failed. She encouraged them to talk to each other, to pull together as a team.

If there is to be shared responsibility, how is this going to come about? The manager is the key person in creating an environment of shared responsibility.

ENCOURAGING SHARED RESPONSIBILITY

What things does a manager need to do to encourage shared responsibility? How can you help members of the work unit to achieve interdependence and true teamwork? Several alternatives are available:

- Give assignments which require unit members to work together in cooperation to complete a task.
- Create opportunities for unit members to assist each other in completing tasks.
- Help unit members to see the unique abilities in each other and to recognize each other's limitations.
- Create a reward system which gives members a greater stake in what the work unit as a whole achieves rather than in what they achieve individually.

One of the most important ways to encourage shared responsibility is to share information and to establish a climate that encourages precisely that. This includes communication between the manager and team members as well as from team member to team member. For example, you might share with team members performance or financial data that previously was shared only with upper management. Or you might encourage your team members to share with members of another department information that was previously kept "in house."

Another way to encourage shared responsibility is to reward it when it takes place. If you expect people to take on more responsibility, they must feel there is something in it for them to do so. You might, for example, include a bonus for team members when a team goal is met.

A third way to encourage shared responsibility is to inform them of the whole-group task and how their part fits into this whole task. For example, at a project start-up meeting, be certain to communicate the whole plan rather than segmenting the information or concentrating on only the team's area of responsibility.

Yet another way to foster sharing of responsibility is to encourage employees to help each other, to view themselves as members of a team rather than as competitors for raises, advances, or even praise.

Other ways to encourage shared responsibility include providing cross-training, insuring that pertinent information is passed on, admitting when you don't know all the answers, and assigning group members to important assignments.

In a work unit where shared responsibility is encouraged, you can also expect to find employees who show a sense of excitement, who express a feeling of camaraderie, and who feel they are a part of something bigger than what they themselves are responsible for singly. Team members in such an atmosphere are likely to be talking to each other, helping each other, praising each other, and expending much more energy on their individual tasks as well.

In a work unit where shared responsibility is a reality, you, as manager are likely to feel energized, supported, efficient, and effective. Think for a minute about a time when you were really motivated, felt full of energy and were able to make full use of your abilities—to perform at the 110 percent level—when you worked *well,* not just hard. What conditions were present?

You might have felt the *task* was challenging, exciting, crucial, or highly visible. The *goals* might have been clear, exciting, high priority. You probably felt *ownership,* that you had the freedom and automony to proceed on your own, that you didn't constantly have to check with your boss. You might also have felt very *accountable,* responsible for your own outcomes. And, you might have felt like part of a *team,* not wanting to let others down, sensing that they were counting on your contribution.

As you consider the preceding conditions frequently present when workers stretch themselves to their limit, what role did the boss play? The boss is absent or rarely seen, functioning as a resource when needed. In most instances the manager is not a boss, but an integral part of the team. The environment is such that the manager facilitates shared responsibilities so team members help each other stretch as much as the manager does.

For you and your employees to function as a team, it is vital that each team member recognize his or her own strengths and weaknesses and those of the other team members.

IDENTIFYING STRENGTHS AND WEAKNESSES

To identify strengths and weaknesses, you might ask your team members to think about times when they have had enjoyable work experience achievements and to identify four to six abilities that recurred in at least half of those achievements. They might select from among the following:

Administer/Maintain
Analyze/Evaluate
Assemble/Make
Build Relationships

Control/Schedule
Convince/Persuade
Coordinate/Act as Liaison
Counsel/Advise
Create/Shape
Design/Draw
Develop/Build
Do/Execute
Formulate/Theorize
Implement/Follow Up
Innovate/Improvise
Interview/Investigate
Learn/Study
Observe/Comprehend
Operate/Run
Organize/Put Together
Perform/Entertain
Plan/Schedule
Practice/Perfect
Promote/Publish
Research/Experiment
Scheme/Strategize
Synthesize/Harmonize
Systematize/Proceduralize
Teach/Train/Speak
Write/Communicate

Next, ask your team members to identify two or three types of subject matter that have recurred in many of the achievements using the following list adapted to your own situation:

Art/Design
Controls/Budgets/Schedules
Efficiency/Productivity
Enterprise/Business
Figures/Details
Graphics/Decoration
Hardware/Equipment
Ideas/Concepts
Living Things
Methods/Procedures
Money/Profits
Needs/Causes
New Things or Ideas
Organization/Group Activity
People Relationships
Physical/Structural Things
Policy/Strategy
Projects/Programs
Stress Circumstances
Systems
Technical (Mechanical, Electrical, Chemical)
Words/Language/Symbols

Next, ask your team members to select two or three circumstances which have recurred in many of the achievements. (Note the overlap between some of the subject matter and circumstances.)

Competition/Test
Constraints/Deadlines

Enterprise/Business
Growth Opportunity/Potential
Methods/Procedures
Needs/Causes
New/Novel Situation
Organization/Group Activity
Projects/Program
Stress Circumstances
Structural Situation
Trouble/Difficulty

Next, ask your team members to select one way of operating with people that recurred in those achievements where they were free to function with others as they desired:

Coach
Coordinator
Director
Individualist
Manager
Team Leader
Team Member

Finally, ask your team members to select the one result which they recall as being consistently present in their achievements:

Acquire/Possess
Apply/Actualize/Realize
Be in Charge/Command
Develop/Build

Discover/Learn
Excel/Be the Best
Exploit/Achieve Potential
Gain Response/Gratitude
Gain Recognition
Improve/Do Better
Make Grade/Fulfill Expectations
Master/Perfect
Organize/Operate
Overcome/Combat
Pioneer/Explore
Serve/Help
Shape/Influence/Control
Stand Out/Be Key/Be Special

By having team members identify individual abilities, subject matter expertise, circumstances fostering achievement, effective ways of interacting with people, and the types of results they most frequently obtain, you can capitalize on each team member's strengths.

TAPPING YOUR TEAM'S FULL POTENTIAL

Cohen and Bradford describe some untapped resources they refer to as the *Four I's* team members may possess: information, initiative, innovation, and implementation.

Information. Team members may know more than you. They may have technical knowledge or knowledge about customers; they may be aware of inside information, both sideways and downward. They may also have knowledge or awareness of developing problems.

Initiative. Often employees cannot wait to be told what to do. They need to be able to meet customers' demands, to solve problems as they arise, to go beyond the assignment, to sense how to "go that extra mile."

Innovation. Some innovations can and must come from within. As noted by Rosabeth Kanter *(The Change Masters)*, how companies are organized affects how innovative they are. Much innovation must come from the middle of the organization and below. Employees at these levels are in a position to spot opportunities and to start new activities.

Implementation. Some great plans never come to fruition because of benign neglect. Employees need enthusiastic commitment to carry out ideas.

Sharing responsibility is one way to assure that you tap your team's full potential, that the team uses all available information, takes the initiative, is innovative, and implements these innovations.

THE SHARED-RESPONSIBILITY TEAM IN ACTION

Before continuing, stop to consider the attribute of shared responsibility and its characteristics in the high-performance team. Locate where you think your work unit is, and if it falls short of the team level, assess which of the possible actions suggested might make sense for your work unit. (See Figure 1.)

Teams with little shared responsibility have unclear individual roles, and team members feel responsible only for completing individual tasks. The leader is seen as the only one to benefit from group success.

Teams with an average amount of shared responsibility have clear individual roles, and team members see how each other's work contributes to the team's success.

Phase	Characteristics	Possible Actions
Team: (81 to 100)	• While members have primary areas of responsibility, they assume other roles as well.	• Support members in their development of new capabilities.
	• Members help each other acquire new skills.	• Reinforce those that help others develop their skills.
	• Members benefit from group as well as individual accomplishments.	• Link rewards to both individual and group performance.
Group: (61 to 80)	• Individual roles are clearly understood by all members.	• Encourage members to serve in new roles on projects.
	• Members understand how each other's work contributes to the group's success.	• Help members learn new skills from one another.
	• Members benefit from individual contributions to the group.	• Reinforce members for group as well as individual success.
Collection: (0 to 60)	• Individual roles are unclear.	• Support members in defining meaningful roles within the group.
	• Members feel responsible for completing specific tasks.	• Help members understand how their work contributes to the group's accomplishments.
	• Leader is perceived as the only one to benefit from group success.	• Provide members with rewards for their individual contributions.

Figure 1 Shared responsibility—feeling personally responsible for the success of the group.

Teams with a large amount of shared responsibility have primary areas of responsibility, but members also assume other roles as well. Members help each other acquire new skills, and members benefit from group as well as from individual accomplishments.

A vision without a task is but a dream, a task without a vision is drudgery, a vision and a task is the hope of the world.

—*1730, a church in Sussex, England*

"If you can dream it, you can do it."

—*Walt Disney*

4

Aligned on Purpose: Sharing a Vision

Ask Yourself . . .

- Are your employees personally committed to fulfilling a purpose?
- Do they see group practices as consistent with that purpose?
- Do they reference this purpose in decision making?
- Do they describe their role in terms of an activity or an outcome?

Supreme Court Justice Oliver Wendell Holmes, a habitual train rider, was aboard a train one day and unable to locate his ticket. The conductor waited patiently while the Chief Justice searched first through his pockets, then through his briefcase. As Justice Holmes became more and more agitated, the conductor said calmly, "Never mind, Sir. We know you. I'm sure the ticket will show up, and you can just mail it to the railroad." At this Mr. Holmes responded, "You don't understand. I'm not worried about finding the ticket for you. The problem is where am I going?"

If you don't know where you're going, you'll never know when you get there. It's like having a gun all loaded and nowhere to shoot—or worse—everywhere to shoot.

WHAT IS PURPOSE?

A key requirement of a high-performance team is that all members share in the same purpose. The purpose must be outside of and apart from the existence and growth of the team itself, and it must fit within the larger purposes of the organization as a whole. Purpose is different from the specific business goals of a work unit or team.

Purpose is a consciously chosen and clearly articulated direction which uses the talents and abilities of your team, contributes to the organization, and leads to a sense of fulfillment for the team members.

Purpose answers the questions "Why do we exist?" "What's our reason for being?" We long for a sense of purpose, to feel we make a difference. We need a good reason to get up each day. Richard Leider in *The Power of Purpose* speaks of "the rust-out syndrome," where our daily work doesn't call forth much energy; life and work have little meaning. People get up because the alarm clock rings; they go to work because it's Monday.

One clear example of purpose is the moving story of Terry Fox. Two days before his eighteenth birthday Terry learned he had cancer and would lose a leg. Rather than indulging in self-pity, Terry shifted his focus from his limitations to his potential and, despite the shock and speed with which his life was turned upside down, he found a personal reason to live. The crisis gave such a strong sense of purpose he was able to perform an extraordinary feat; with an artificial leg, he ran over 3300 miles across Canada (the equivalent of a marathon a day) to raise money for cancer research. His goal was to raise one million dollars. Terry ran until he could run no more. His Marathon of Hope inspired people to contribute over 30 million dollars. Although Terry died, his spirit, his sense of purpose endures. Since his death thousands of Canadians have run each year to raise money for cancer research.

Organizations, like individuals, also need a good reason for being. As author Peter Drucker argues, every organization must ask itself, "What business are we in? What's our true purpose?" Organizations need a purpose that goes beyond surviving, growing, or making a profit. They need to do something in a special way.

Charles Garfield, in *Secrets of Super Achievers,* notes that: "Workaholics are addicted to activity; super-achievers are committed to results. . . . Peak performers want more than merely to win the next game. They see all the way to the championship. They have a long-range goal that inspires commitment and action." He tells of 40-year-old Thomas Watson who was made general manager of a small company that made meat slicers, time clocks, and primitive tabulators called punch cards. He saw the potential of the punch cards and renamed his little business International Business Machines Corporation. When asked years later at what point in his career he envisioned IBM becoming so big, he answered, "Right at the beginning."

A. David Silver (*Entrepreneurial Megabucks*) describes the purposes of those he considers the 100 greatest entrepreneurs of the last 25 years. Included were the following:

> Henry Bloch recognized the growing complexity of income tax forms in the mid-1950s and believed that a trustworthy, careful tax preparation service with a national reputation could be successful. . . . The solution: H & R Bloch.

> Frank L. Carney . . . [believed] people wanted a quick meal, nice atmosphere, and moderate prices. In the 1960s he gave them pizza [Pizza Hut]. In the 1980s with his second venture, Chi-Chi's, Carney is giving them a family-style restaurant serving Mexican food and alcoholic beverages.

> Leonard Samuel Shoen . . . perceived the need for Americans to be able to move their belongings from place to place, simply, inexpensively, and without hiring professional movers. The solution: the U-Haul System.

> Charles Kemmons Wilson . . . After a 1951 family vacation to Washington, D.C., Wilson realized the need for providing affordable, convenient, comfortable lodging to the hordes of traveling Americans taking to the nation's highways. The solution: a successful formula of standardized rooms, quality control, reasonable prices, and family accommodations conveniently located near major travel arteries is what made Holiday Inns the largest motor-hotel chain in the world.

Harold Geneen, mastermind of the growth of ITT and manager of its 350 companies notes that no matter what a person is managing—a business or a home—the test is always the same: "whether or not it achieves the goals it sets for itself; the higher the goals, the better the management" *(Managing)*. Likewise consultant Roger Fritz *(Rate Yourself as a Manager)* suggests managers need to ask key questions such as: "Do I have a compelling vision, a mental image of what I want to accomplish? Do I keep that goal in sight—for my staff and myself. Do I concentrate? Do I focus attention and energy on my goals?"

This is in direct contrast to the manager described by Edward Wakin ("Management strategy: Tackle those goals!"):

> A manager was thought to be ideal for his new appointment as vice president of a high-tech firm. His credentials were excellent: He was a technical expert but also had a strong sense of human relations.
>
> Several months later, however, members of his staff complained that they weren't able to get their job done. They had begun to call their new manager the butterfly, because he flitted from one situation to another. He never zeroed in on any project or set priorities.
>
> Whatever his qualifications, this executive failed to achieve his bottom-line responsibility: getting results. The best managers, like the best leaders, pick a target, evaluate their resources, plan their strategy and then aim at the bull's eye.

Bennis and Nanus warn against "organizational vertigo and myopia," explaining that the larger an organization becomes, the greater the number of images or purposes the organization may have. For example: "Starting with a strong base in radio, television, and communications, RCA had drifted into such diverse fields as auto rental and financial services under a succession of presidents, until it had become nearly paralyzed by conflicting images of where it should be headed."

PURPOSE VS. GOAL

What is the distinction between a goal and a purpose? A purpose is an ongoing, general direction, whereas a goal has a beginning, middle, and end. It is a specific target. A goal that fits under the purpose is "on purpose." A purpose is like an umbrella under which fit the specific goals the team chooses, as illustrated in Figure 1.

THE IMPORTANCE OF PURPOSE

Now that you've seen the distinction between a purpose and a goal, consider why purpose is important. People understand the value and importance of business goals. Yet not everyone may

PURPOSE: To Develop and Maintain the Highest Quality Coating Process

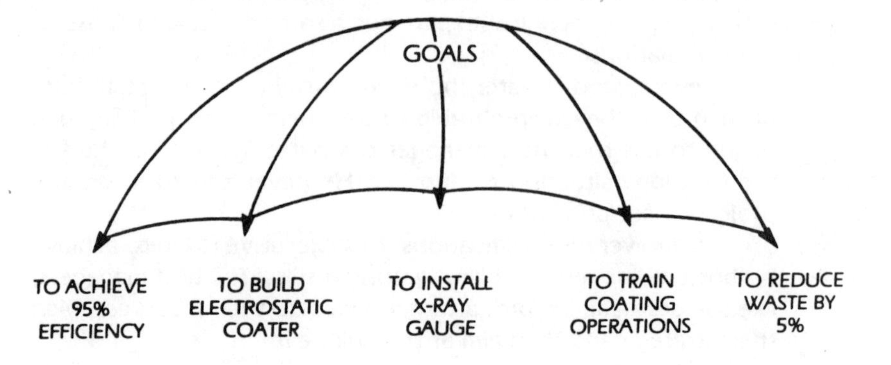

PURPOSE:

1. Consciously chosen and clearly articulated
2. Ongoing general direction
3. Uses the talents of your team
4. Contributes to the company as a whole
5. Leads to a sense of fulfillment for team members

GOALS:

1. A specific target that is measurable
2. Has a beginning, middle, and end
3. Fits under the purpose

Figure 1 Purpose vs. goals.

understand the significance of purpose as it relates to the energy people may be willing to devote to their jobs.

For starters—why do you work? One obvious answer is money in order to support yourself financially. Economic necessity is at the base of most people's motivation to work. But more often than not, people are also looking for more in a job than just a paycheck.

A study once asked people: "If you had as much money as you wanted, would you still work?" Ninety percent of the people said they would. In response to a second question, "Would you stay in your current job?" ninety percent said they would *not* work in their current job. When those people were asked what kind of work they wanted to do, most said they wanted to work with people, to make a contribution, to do something meaningful for others.

This study implies that people work for many reasons, but one issue that is important to them is a sense of meaning. Having a clear purpose can help people with that sense of meaning. Most people have a strong desire to do something that makes a difference, that makes a contribution. They want to experience satisfaction and fulfillment in the process of working. A job may have many negatives—having to be gone on weekends, attending boring meetings, working with unlikeable clients—but if an employee has bought into the job, he or she will do these things willingly, knowing they are part of the territory. If, on the other hand, there is no sense of purpose, the employee may resent the negatives associated with the job.

THE FUNCTIONS OF PURPOSE

Purpose serves at least four important functions for high-performance teams in most organizations.

First, purpose gives a *context for decision making,* a stable point of reference from which to set goals and make plans. Jack Morton, Bell Labs, said of the importance of purpose:

> The innovation process also must have a well-understood social purpose. This purpose must answer the question: "Why are we innovating?" And the answer must say more than just "We want to grow." or "We want to be more profitable." Moreover, the purpose of the organization must permeate the *whole* industrial enterprise; all who work in the organization must understand what the organization is for.

Consider, for example, Pizza Hut's desire to provide a "quick meal." This precludes some menu items, but makes the "personal pan pizza in 5 minutes" a very viable objective.

Second, purpose provides a *yardstick,* making possible a measurement of the progress of the team relative to an external standard. Recall J.F. Kennedy's goal of putting a man on the moon by 1970. On July 20, 1969, Americans heard Neil Armstrong announce from the Sea of Tranquility on the moon: "The Eagle has landed." In this instance J.F.K. accomplished his goal.

Third, purpose provides a *focus for collaboration and shared responsibility.* Work is becoming increasingly interdependent as teams form around specific problems and a variety of expertise must be brought to bear. Managers sometimes do not have the expertise to solve the problems of the work unit and must tap the greater expertise of members of the work unit. The importance of the opportunity for collaboration and shared responsibility given a purpose is seen in A. David Silver's description of how the founders of Apple Computer got together:

> Jobs and Wozniak met in 1975 when Jobs was a video game designer at Atari, where founder Nolan Bushnell wanted to reduce the number of chips in his Pong game from 150–170 to less than 40. Wozniak, then an engineer at Hewlett-Packard Company, had designed a version of Pong that used about 30 chips. Bushnell told Jobs and Wozniak that he would give them $700 if they could design "Breakout," a Pong upgrade, with less than 50 chips, and $1,000 if it was under 40 chips. Wozniak and Jobs delivered a breadboard model in four days with 44 chips.

Fourth, purpose is a *motivator for excellence and high performance.* It unites employees, making them willing to give up pettiness in the pursuit of higher goals. It focuses energy on outcomes—the whole rather than segmented pieces. It satisfies the need of those workers who want to make a difference. People want to believe in something that brings out the best in them, something that taps their *energy of the spirit.*

Of the 90 leaders interviewed by Bennis and Nanus, every one had:

> . . . an *agenda,* an unparalleled concern with outcome. Leaders are the most results-oriented individuals in the world, and results get attention. Their visions or intentions are compelling and pull people toward them. Intensity coupled with commitment is magnetic. And these intense personalities do not have to coerce people to pay attention; they are so intent on what they are doing that, like a child completely absorbed with creating a sand castle in a sandbox, they draw others in.

A strong sense of purpose stimulates the release of energy of the spirit, focusing attention on what you want rather than what you don't want. You've probably seen demonstrations of a martial arts expert breaking a pile of boards with his bare hands. He's trained to focus his attention not on the boards, but to concentrate his energy where the bottom board meets the table. Good tennis players and golfers are taught to hit *through* the ball—to think of where they want the ball to go. Being dominated by *fear* of what you don't want, rather than being led by purpose, can have negative consequences.

The Wallenda Effect

One of the most graphic examples of the consequences of fear of failure is the tragic death of tightrope aerialist Karl Wallenda. In 1968 Wallenda stated: "Being on the tightrope is living; everything else is waiting." He had a clear sense of purpose, had bought into his vocation totally. Ten years later he fell to his death. His wife, also an aerialist, reported that in his later years Karl became increasingly preoccupied with not falling. He started supervising the setups and checked and rechecked the guide wires, something he had not done in a long while. This was quite unlike his earlier years when all his energy was focused on succeeding, not on avoiding a fall.

This same phenomenon is readily apparent in sports when a winning team starts playing to keep its lead rather than to increase it. A team playing not to lose rather than to win frequently loses momentum and the opponent, focused on winning, uses its positive energy to turn the game around.

Individuals and organizations who are purpose focused do not see setbacks as failures; rather they see them as learning experiences. Take, for example, the behavior of Tom Watson, IBMs founder and leader, when he learned that a promising young junior executive had engaged in a risky business venture that lost over $10 million dollars. He called the man into his office, and when the young executive asked if Watson wanted him to resign, Watson replied, "You can't be serious. We've just spent $10 million dollars educating you."

ALIGNED ON PURPOSE

Having alignment on purpose means the group members are *committed* to the direction and outcome of the group. They are committed to the part their group plays in helping the overall organization achieve success. There is a connection between the amount and kind of energy (energy of the spirit) they put forth and their alignment to the purpose of the work unit.

This does not mean that everyone is in total agreement with the purpose. Alignment means that while there may be differing points of view, members are willing to set those differences aside in pursuit of a common purpose or goal.

Think about a time when you were part of a group with real purpose. What was the purpose of the group and how did you feel? Consider a contrasting situation when you were part of a group with no common purpose, that was spinning its wheels, accomplishing little or nothing. How did that feel? Compare your feelings to those that are predictable, listed below:

Common Purpose	No Common Purpose
• Work beyond $ only, work for a cause	• Work for $ only
• Find satisfaction in work	• Find satisfaction outside of work (often while *at* work)
• Important to put in time *and* energy	• Important to put in time
• Important to know how their contribution adds to the organization	• Not sure or don't have high interest in how their contribution adds to the organization
• Describe work in terms of outcomes	• Describe work in terms of activity

In short, the whole tone of living goes up for individuals with purpose because there is more meaning attached to what they do. Many events in history illustrate groups of people with a strong sense of purpose and the extraordinary things they were able to accomplish: the small number of immigrants to the United States pioneering our great nation; the coming together of Americans during the world wars (in contrast to the divisiveness of the Vietnam war).

In a closer-to-home-example, imagine you encounter three men who are laying bricks, and you ask each what he is doing. The first man replies, "Making $12 an hour laying these bricks." The second man answers, "Building a wall." And the third man states, "Creating a cathedral so people can worship." It's the third man who would get up eagerly and go to work, not because it was Monday, but because the cathedral needed to be completed. Carry the example further and imagine how each of these men would react if the wall was off by a few degrees. The first bricklayer would probably ignore it; the second would probably report it to the boss; the third would probably fix it.

Another example that illustrates the importance of purpose in making a difference is that of the three umpires who are discussing balls and strikes. The first umpire says, "There are balls and there are strikes, and I calls 'em like I sees 'em." The second umpire says, "Well, I calls 'em like they is." The third umpire says, "You're both wrong, they ain't nothing 'til we calls 'em."

GETTING ALIGNED ON PURPOSE

If feeling a sense of purpose is so important, why is it so uncommon in the work force? One reason people may not feel their work is purposeful is because the purpose is established by others and handed down to them. Or the purpose may not be clarified at the work unit level. Simply telling employees what you believe the purpose is most likely will not be effective. People are more likely to be committed to a purpose that *they* have had some opportunity to help establish. However, developing a statement of purpose with team member input is not easy. The following process was developed to help provide managers with a practical tool to use team member input in developing a purpose statement. One team member reported after his team went through this process that "we made more progress with this process in one hour and a half than any other attempt we've made at developing a purpose statement."

Developing a Purpose Statement

1. Ask input from team members. It is important to solicit input from team members about the purpose of the work unit. Have them think about the things the unit does well. What contribution do they make to the organization that no one else can do as well? What has the unit done in the past that made the members feel good? What is the most important thing for the unit to focus on in the future? What do they want out of their jobs? What would the company lose if the unit left? What makes them special? Unique? Questions such as these can help get your team members thinking. You probably have other questions to include during the input phase of purpose statement development.

2. Incubate the input. Once you have input from your group, don't try to write the purpose statement immediately. Let the ideas incubate for a while to give you and the group a chance to step back and think about the ideas that have been put forth. This also reduces the pressure to come up with something quickly that will satisfy everyone.

3. Write a draft purpose statement and submit it to team members. The purpose statement should take into account your sense of the purpose for the team as well as the team members' ideas. Look for common themes that represent your group's thoughts. Don't worry about coming up with the perfect statement the first time around. You'll be reviewing it with your team to get their reactions and comments, so don't propose it as etched-in-stone. In fact, your purpose should never be etched-in-stone, but rather periodically should be reviewed and changed if circumstances have changed.

4. Discuss the draft statement with team members. Ask for their reactions, ideas for improvement, and input for change. By doing this, you are using the purpose statement as a starting point, but getting team involvement for the final version. This involvement is a critical step toward gaining alignment and commitment from your team members. It is also the most difficult step in the process. Key manager behaviors in this step include insuring that all viewpoints come out, looking for commonality among differing points, listening for rationales behind positions or favorite words, and trying to negotiate a win/win situation with the team. Bennis and Nanus suggest that:

> If there is a spark of genius in the leadership function at all, it must lie in this transcending ability, a kind of magic, to assemble—out of all the variety of images, signals, forecasts and

alternatives—a clearly articulated vision of the future that is at once simple, easily understood, clearly desirable, and energizing.

5. Write a final purpose statement with the consensus of the team members. Through discussion with your team about their reactions and changes to your draft statement, reword the statement to reflect both your and the team members' sense of purpose. Everyone may not agree 100 percent with each word, but it is important to strive for a statement people can buy into.

6. Solicit statements of commitment from team members. An important last step is to ask for verbal commitment from the team members regarding the statement.

A statement of purpose derived using the described process has a high probability of aligning your team members with a common purpose. Your statement should be more than words on paper. It should be visually displayed and kept in front of you and your team. It should be continually referred to as the team sets goals and measures progress toward those goals.

A PURPOSE-ORIENTED TEAM IN ACTION

Take a few minutes to see how purpose oriented your people are. Are their behaviors in this area characteristic of a collection of individuals, a group, or a team?

A work unit scoring low in terms of purpose oriented is unclear about the unit's purpose; therefore purpose is not considered in decision making or in determining the appropriateness of group practices. A work unit scoring in the average range understands the unit's purpose but lacks commitment to it. They may use it occasionally in decision making and in determining the appropriateness of group practices. A work unit scoring high on purpose orientation has members personally committed to the unit's purpose. They use this purpose in decision making and in evaluating group practices.

Phase	Characteristics	Possible Actions
Team: (81 to 100)	• Members feel personally committed to fulfilling their purpose. • Members reference the purpose in making decisions. • Members see group practices that are consistent with the group's purpose.	• Review the group's purpose periodically to update and/or recommit. • Reinforce decisions that support the group's purpose. • Reinforce practices of the consequences for achieving or failing to achieve the group's purpose.
Group: (61 to 80)	• Members understand the purpose, but lack strong commitment to it. • Members begin referencing the purpose when making decisions. • Members see some group practices as being inconsistent with the group's purpose.	• Facilitate discussions of the consequences for achieving or failing to achieve the group's purpose. • Encourage members to consider the purpose when making decisions. • Help the group change inconsistent practices and/or redefine the purpose.
Collection: (0 to 60)	• Members are unclear about the group's purpose. • Decision making is done without regard to a group purpose. • Members have no effective way to determine the appropriateness of group practices.	• Clarify your perception of the group's purpose and ask for input. • Ask members how specific decisions will help the group. • Facilitate discussions about group practices that help and hinder the group.

Figure 2 Alignment on purpose—having a shared vision which gives work meaning.

If language be not in accordance with the truth of things, affairs cannot be carried on to success.

—*Confucius*

Can we talk?

—*Joan Rivers*

5

High Communication: Building Trust

Ask Yourself . . .

- Do your employees give each other constructive feedback?
- Are they open to receiving feedback?
- Is communication open, empathic, and solution-oriented?
- Are members responding to information in ways that stop people from talking?
- Do members trust each other? You?

In the mid 1960s General Motors launched its new compact Chevrolet Nova in the Mexican market. Sales were appalling. The reason was discovered when an employee who spoke Spanish commented that in Spanish "no va" means "it doesn't go."

Messages often *do* get lost in translation. In another case Sol Linowitz, ambassador to the Organization of American States and former chairman of the Xerox Corporation, met with a group of Central American presidents. One president asked about Linowitz's old company. He explained briefly what the Xerox company did, and the interpreter translated the explanation into Spanish. The group began talking with one another in great animation and apparent incredulity and then quieted, awe-struck, waiting in eager anticipation for what he would say next. Concerned, Linowitz asked the interpreter exactly what he had said. The interpreter answered, "I told them just what you said—that Xerox is a company that has invented a new method of reproduction."

THE TRADITIONAL APPROACH

Traditionally, members of the work unit depend on the manager for direction, information, and ideas. Thus communication is primarily one-way between the manager and the members of the work unit, and it is usually one-on-one communication. Keep this assumption about communication in mind as you read this chapter.

SATISFACTION, COMMUNICATION, AND PERFORMANCE

For many years researchers have looked for a correlation between satisfaction and performance. They have researched satisfaction about self, job, peers, management, and organizations. They found that a person could be satisfied with all of these and still not perform well.

The breakthrough came when satisfaction was correlated to *communication.* The results of this research can be summarized as follows:

Satisfaction	Communication	Performance
high	high	highest
low	high	high
high	low	low
low	low	lowest

From this research it can be concluded that employees who were satisfied and talked about it performed the best; employees who were dissatisfied and didn't talk about it performed the worst. They probably used their energy to remain hidden. These are findings you might expect. Surprisingly, however, those who were satisfied but didn't talk about it were ranked lower in overall performance than those who were dissatisfied but talked about it. What does this mean? Even people who may not be fully satisfied but have an environment where they can *communicate* about their dissatisfaction perform better than those who may be satisfied but are in a climate lacking open communication.

Given these findings, what is management's responsibility when it comes to creating high performance? Clearly, *communication* is critical to high performance. The more frequently employees communicate, the more likely they will perform well. Therefore, a primary responsibility of a manager is to encourage communication and participation.

The keys to this study are *communication* and *satisfaction.* People who experience both perform better. But even people who are dissatisfied perform better, if given the opportunity to communicate, than those who are satisfied but do not talk. One possible explanation for this phenomenon is that words transmit energy. What you say has the potential to energize others. What you say also creates internal commitment. Managers who can create and maintain high communication in their work units have discovered one way to stimulate the release of *synergy.* Synergy is the condition when every member of the team is transmitting positive energy in ways which build on each other to produce an effect greater than the simple sum of the energy inputs (2 + 2 = 5).

If high communication leads to synergy, what leads to high communication? Think about that. Who do you communicate openly with? Those you *trust.* Trust is a prerequisite to high communication. When you do not trust someone, you are unwilling to communicate with them. The major *no trust* issue is that people *stop communicating.* If communication stops, several negative consequences can occur, including confusion, tension, reduction of productivity, resentment, frustration, and inability of employees to do the job. How can this be prevented?

THE PINCH MODEL

The Pinch Model (Figure 1) illustrates the importance of maintaining effective communication and the consequences for failing to do so.

When a team first comes together, it is important for the manager to establish *expectations* on two fronts:

1. Tasks—what each member of the team is to do on the job and
2. Relationships—how they are going to relate to each other.

It is critical to gain *agreement* on the *roles* of the group members. This is true for both agreeing what tasks need to be accomplished and by whom, and gaining agreement on expectations for interpersonal communication. When you are looking at how a team functions, it is extremely important to be clear about how the team will communicate with each other.

Agreement should produce relative *stability* between the manager and team members, and among the team members themselves. The length of time that stability continues depends on the amount and kinds of changes that occur.

Changes are inevitable in a work environment. Some changes are small, hardly noticed, and easily dealt with. Other changes have more of an impact. Changes can eventually lead to a *pinch,* a small problem or interpersonal disturbance between individuals. A pinch is a situation in which an individual or individuals feel something is wrong. It's not a full-blown problem or crisis—*yet.* A pinch may occur because of missed expectations, failure to deal with demands outside the group, or because the manager changes the rules. It may result from an increase in

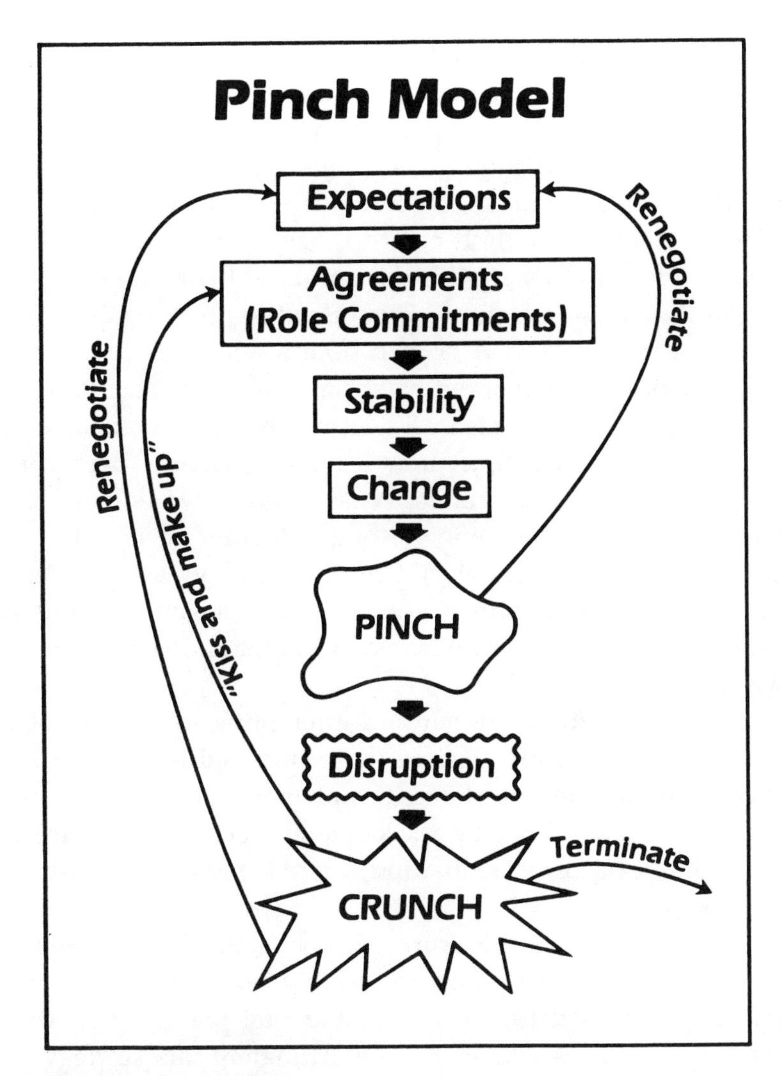

Figure 1 The Pinch model.

workload, schedule changes, inappropriate delivery of feedback, lack of needed support, or failure to keep an agreement or commitment. Or it may arise from a misunderstanding between two people about their job responsibilities. It may occur if a team member fails to communicate that he or she is behind an expected schedule and the fact is discovered in a team meeting. It may also occur if a team member violates an agreement, but fails to communicate this openly. Whatever it is, *now* is the time to handle the pinch and to renegotiate expectations.

One pinch by itself may not be all that damaging, but, if a pinch is not dealt with, it can fester and get worse; it can turn into a series of pinches with disruption of the relationships between the people involved. This disruption may continue until it results in a *crunch.* A crunch occurs when the problem becomes serious. It is marked by strong emotional reactions from both sides. This may mean a heated discussion or total avoidance. Think, for example, how a highly assertive person may choose to deal with a crunch. What behavior would you expect to see? Attacking, blaming, getting autocratic in how to fix it, and the like (fight behavior)? Think about how a low assertive person might deal with a crunch. What behavior would you expect to see? Withdrawal, avoidance, quit and stay, (flight behavior)?

Dealing with a crunch and attempting to *renegotiate* expectations is difficult because those involved tend to be emotional, options become limited, and managers feel they must follow discipline procedures. People get locked into their positions, and it becomes a situation where someone must win and someone lose.

One option at the crunch point is the *kiss-and-make-up* strategy, agreeing to return to stability without discussing the issues that caused the crunch in the first place. Often this is seen as a positive action, but unfortunately this strategy provides a false sense of security. Failure to deal with the problems that caused the crunch result in a high probability that you will return to the crunch very quickly.

Another option at the crunch point is *termination.* You may terminate or transfer the individuals involved. Or they may decide to quit and leave—or quit and stay. Those who have quit and stayed exhibit identifiable behavior such as a drop in performance, failure to contribute in meetings, negative attitudes, stealing time, and refusal to carry out their responsibilities as team members.

To better understand the Pinch Model, imagine the following scenario.

> Melonie has called her team together to discuss their schedule and all the work they have to accomplish in the next few months. She stresses that they will have to pull together and work as a team, which means a high level of communication, both between them and her and among each other. She also stresses that anything that becomes a problem or issue for them should be brought to the group so they can resolve it. The team members nod in agreement.
>
> Melonie continues, "Even though you'll be working independently, every phase of this project will, in the end, need to be integrated, so any changes made by one of you will affect the rest of the group. Therefore, if you make any changes, let the rest of us know so we can determine what adjustments we might need to make. I'll try not to throw any of you anything you can't handle, but let me know if there's something you need help with." Again the team members nod and express agreement.

In the context of the Pinch Model, the expectations and role agreements are that there will be tight deadlines and a high need to communicate, that they will bring up their problems, and that they will share changes with each other.

Over the next few weeks stability is demonstrated by team members sharing information and the team members keeping each other and Melonie informed of changes.

> One day Melonie decides Phase 3 of the project is moving too slowly, so she pulls Stan's people off finalizing design reports and assigns them to Phase 3. The next day she reassigns Fred's group to Phase 4. Both protest the reassignments, but Melonie insists that's the only way they can meet their deadline. That same day she calls a meeting to discuss their progress, and George asks to discuss a change he wants to make with the circuit board defluxing. When Melonie asks if it's a priority concern, he says it isn't, but that it will affect everyone down the

line, and he'd like to anticipate any problems they might have to address. Melonie expresses her appreciation to George for looking to the future, but then says: "We have a lot to worry about right now, without jumping off on problems that might never happen. Let's just keep in the direction we're going and see what happens."

She then asks if anyone else has any changes—changes with immediate impact. The group is non-responsive, so Melonie adjourns the meeting.

Over the next few days the team continues to get further behind schedule, so Melonie calls them together saying, "What we're faced with now is really pretty simple. We're behind schedule. What we need to do is talk about how we got here and what's causing the delays. Would anyone care to comment?"

The group is non-responsive. As Melonie keeps pressing them for reasons, Stan finally suggests that one reason has been all the reassignments they've had to deal with. When Melonie asks why they didn't bring that up before, Stan says the reassignments didn't seem open to discussion. To this Melonie angrily responds, "What? Not open for discussion? At the beginning of this project, I told all of you that we were to bring problems and questions here." The members of the group shift uneasily in their chairs and make no response.

In the context of the Pinch Model, the pinches were caused by reassignment of responsibilities and failure to address issues brought up by team members.

The crunch occurred when the team members got behind schedule and became unwilling to participate in the meeting. The team moved back to a manager-focus with Melonie doing most of the talking and all of the decision making. The group passively waits to be told what to do next.

Dealing with Pinches

It's easy to recognize a pinch and say, "It's not that big a deal." At that point, it may not be, but it is important to realize the consequences of failing to deal with pinches.

To encourage people to communicate, it is vital to create an atmosphere in which they recognize that you are willing to listen to and handle situations at the pinch point, rather than an atmosphere in which you communicate only when necessary. Being in a climate where problems are dealt with at the pinch level instead of the crunch level may be very different from what many people have experienced.

How you establish the expectation that pinches are to be dealt with is a critical element of team communication. Think about what a manager needs to do to establish the expectation of sharing and dealing with pinches. How can you create a climate where the expectation is to share and deal openly with problems?

You might explain the Pinch Model, provide examples of pinches so the group sees what you mean, give them permission to share them, listen when they do, and act on legitimate pinches.

Getting people to share and deal with pinches does not happen automatically. People need to understand and believe that it is not only the expectation, but that there is something in it for them to share pinches.

PERMISSION, PROTECTION, POTENCY

The following simple three-step process can encourage your team members to share their pinches and create effective communication.

Permission. People need to be given permission to assert themselves and take the first step. It needs to be clear to them that it is all right to share a pinch they are having, rather than feeling it is inappropriate. It is important for managers to ask for pinches. You might establish the practice of having team members say, "I have a pinch," which is then immediately recognized as a stop point to talk.

Protection. People need to feel safe in asserting themselves. Let people know that if they do share a pinch, you won't discount their feelings or react negatively to their assertions. You don't have to agree with their pinch, but you should acknowledge it, thank them for their openness, and discuss the problem. If someone shares a pinch and feels punished because they did, they will think twice before sharing another one.

Potency. People also need to feel that sharing a pinch will make a difference. Potency here means some action is taken to deal with and resolve the pinch. If someone shares a pinch and nothing is done to resolve the situation, people will feel that sharing pinches makes no difference, and they will not be willing to share pinches in the future.

To illustrate the permission, protection, potency process, consider a situation in which a pinch exists because of a misunderstanding about job responsibilities. The person should understand that the team and the team goal will suffer if the confusion continues. The manager should point out that it is *appropriate* to discuss this pinch which may be nothing more than a small misunderstanding. If, however, the person expressing confusion over job responsibility senses that the supervisor or the team reacts uninterested or negatively, the person is unlikely to discuss this or any other pinch in the future. In contrast, if an immediate clarification of job responsibility is made for a person who has shared his or her pinch and, in turn, if there is rapid follow-up with others to clarify the confusion, this will help to encourage future discussions by all members of the team who are aware of the action taken.

Another example of the permission, protection, potency process involves a team member who violates an agreement with another team member who is rather mild-mannered and nonaggressive (low assertive). The manager notices the withdrawal of this team member whenever he is in the presence of the team member who violated the agreement. The manager gives permission and protection, in private, to uncover the problem. The manager then praises this team member for sharing and encourages him to share problems sooner next time. Immediately after this the manager takes action to alleviate the problem that was uncovered.

This three-step process is not magic, but it is a way to help establish the expectation within a team that the pinch level is where you should deal with issues that affect the team.

To prevent crunches, communication must occur before or at the pinch level. The success/failure of a high-performance team depends on how they handle pinches. It is important that you establish the expectation that the group deal with pinches.

If you typically handle problems only at the crunch point, you are basically saying, "If it's a major problem I'll deal with it, but if it's not, I don't want to hear about it." You are also seen as being in a reactive mode. Such actions quickly lead to a passive group that listens to its manager give directions. Team members will put in their time but minimize their efforts and energy.

In contrast, if you deal with pinches, you are saying that if there's a problem, let's deal with it and move on. You are also seen as being in a proactive mode. Rather than communicating only when it is necessary or unavoidable, you are showing a desire to maintain stability.

The Pinch Model is helpful for dealing with pinches that you see. But in many cases, you are not aware of pinches affecting those who work for you. In those situations, it is critical for team members to feel encouraged to bring their pinches to you. The manner in which you communicate with your employees plays a major role in the level of trust that is present. In some cases, people may have the ability to share information about pinches, but feel that the climate is such that they are unwilling to communicate.

COMMUNICATION-STOPPING BEHAVIORS

An important aspect of whether people are willing to communicate or not is how they are responded to when they attempt to do so. According to Dr. Jack R. Gibb, well-known trainer and author of *Trust: A New View of Personal and Organizational Development,* six behaviors tend to stop communication: judging, superiority, certainty, controlling, manipulation, and indifference.

These behavior modes are often engaged in innocently and unconsciously, certainly not deliberately by well-meaning people. In addition to the actual words that are spoken, the tone of voice and body language can stop communication.

Judging. "You're wrong." Evaluating or judging the other person or his/her ideas results from not listening for ideas or possibilities, but instead discounting the ideas or implying the other person is wrong. For example, during a meeting, Russ Stewart suggests to Andrea that she's probably having problems with deadlines and to Frank that he's probably all snarled up with the Conner's project. When they both concur he states:

> "I could have seen this coming a mile off. You people are going to have to learn to get your priorities straight. You've got to pay more attention to detail."

Superiority. "I'm better than you." Communicating a feeling of superiority in position, power, or ability implies the other person can't be right because of his/her inadequacies. There tends to be a sense of one-upmanship to this approach. For example, Andrea and Frank attempt to defend their position by pointing out that they aren't that far off. Russ's response is:

> "I don't agree, and I've been around here long enough to know. If you'd listened to what I tried to tell you in the beginning, we wouldn't be sitting around here now trying to make sense out of all this."

Certainty. "Don't confuse me with facts. My mind's made up." This communication implies the person knows all the answers and doesn't need or desire any additional information. There is a high need to be right, even to the point of winning an argument rather than solving a problem. There was some of this certainty in the preceding superiority scenario. There is more when Russ makes some assignments to get them back on track, saying:

> "Everybody knows his area of responsibility now, so there shouldn't be any problems."
>
> Frank wants to talk about the new assignments, to which Russ replies, "Frank, we have talked about it, and I've made the decision. By the end of the week I want to see some results."

Controlling. "Let me tell you how to do your job." Controlling is trying to change or restrict someone else's behavior or attitude by imposing a set of values or beliefs on them. A person who engages in this behavior has a high need to be in control of others and the situation. Managers often believe this is their responsibility. For example, in response to Russ's expectation of results by the end of the week, Jerry indicates that without help he won't be able to meet that deadline. Russ responds:

> Why does this always happen. I tried to tell you how to complete this project without running into time problems. Didn't anybody listen to me. Now, what you have to do is clear your calendar and give full attention to this project."

Manipulation. "Gotcha!" Manipulation is communicating with hidden motives in a way that uses others to meet one's own needs. This type of communication has a "gotcha" feel. For example, Russ tells his people that if they can't make the deadline it will put him in a tremendous bind:

> "I'm really counting on you people to bring in the project on deadline. But if you can't handle it—" and he allows a meaningful pause, responded to by the team members saying they can handle it. "That's what I want to hear," Russ proclaims. "I know you can handle it too; that's why you're on the project. Now here's what I think you should do—."

Indifference. "You're not important. What you say doesn't count." Indifference shows a lack of interest or concern for the feelings or welfare of the other person that implies the other person's comments are unimportant. For example, Andrea suggests that she will have a problem making the deadline unless she can get the material from the design department within the next few days.

> Russ has been busily taking notes, but at Andrea's prompting, he replies: "I don't know if I can get design to move any faster. I mean, it's not really my job anyway. Ted's in charge of that. Have any of you seen the latest budget figures on the Germaine project?"
>
> Frank says he thought they came in the morning mail, but he hadn't looked at them. Andrea presses to return to the design problem.
>
> Russ sighs and says, "As you know, they're on a pretty steep ordering curve over there, what with all the new software. It takes time to work things out. Maybe we should wait and see on that. Frank, would you run back to your office and find those budget figures. I'd really like to see them."

Other Communication Stoppers

The preceding behavior modes are often adopted unconsciously. Well-meaning, good-intentioned people too often display such behavior without even realizing it. They may also unconsciously engage in other behavior that will inhibit communication, including facial expressions such as frowning or raising eyebrows, shaking the head, yawning, sighing, leaning back, avoiding eye contact, gazing around the room, taking irrelevant notes, or changing the subject.

COMMUNICATION-ENCOURAGING BEHAVIORS

Dr. Gibb has also identified six behavior modes that encourage communication: description, equality, openness, problem-orientation, positive intent, and empathy. In addition, other actions may also enhance communication.

Description. The opposite of judging. "I see it this way." "How do you see it?" The person applying description is seen as requesting information about ideas in an attempt to more fully understand them. The person presents feelings or perceptions which do not imply that others are wrong or need to change. For example, Russ Stewart says to his team:

> "The way I see it we've got time problems. What you've done is all right for a start, but we have to go on from there. You've given me some useful insights. I have a better understanding of the problems concerning these deadlines. As I see it—." His team members nod in agreement.

Equality. The opposite of superiority. "We're in this together." "I'm glad we have different viewpoints. Since we're on the same team we have a better chance of covering every angle." Communication is enhanced when you treat others with respect and trust. Differences in talent, ability, power, and status often exist, but the person who encourages communication seems to attach little importance to these distractors. For example, Russ continues with: "Let's see if we can come up with some ideas. I have confidence we can work this thing out." Again, his team members voice agreement.

Openness. The opposite of certainty. "What do you see as the key issue here?" "Let's hear your ideas. You're right. That's a better idea." The person with an open attitude is seen as investigating issues rather than taking sides on them, as a problem solver rather than a debater. The person is indicating an interest in a shared approach to solving the problem. Some of this openness is seen in the preceding "equality" scenario. And it is seen as Russ pursues the problem: "We do have time problems, but I'll be honest with you. We can't change the deadline. Can anyone give me some more details on how we got where we are?" Team members begin sharing ideas and isolate three they agree on.

Problem-Orientation. The opposite of controlling. "You know the opportunity, and I'm sure you have the answer."

When a person communicates a desire to work together to define a problem or seek a solution, he or she is seen as asking questions, seeking information, and having no predetermined solution, attitude, or method to impose. Recall the previous scenario when Frank felt he could not meet the deadline. To encourage communication, Russ's response might have been: "All right. Tell me how you feel this could be a problem. We're going to have to work out a solution if there's going to be one."

Positive Intent. The opposite of manipulation. "Can we go back and focus on our common objective for a moment?" "Here are my motives in this case." Behavior that appears to be spontaneous and free of deception encourages communication. If the person is seen as being straightforward and honest, and as behaving spontaneously in response to the situation, he or she is likely to create minimal defensiveness. For example, Russ again explains that not meeting the deadline will really put *them* in a bind, but then, instead of laying a guilt trip on them, he admits it will be tight and asks if there is any way they can make the deadline.

Empathy. The opposite of indifference. "I appreciate your concern. I sense your frustration." "I understand how you feel; I'd feel the same way if I were in your shoes." Empathy reflects feelings and respect for the worth of the other person. The person having empathy identifies with other people's problems, shares feelings, and accepts another's reaction at face value. For example, in response to Andrea's concern about not getting the needed materials for design, Russ might have replied: "I understand how that can slow you down. Is there anything I can do to get design to move any faster?"

Andrea suggests he might talk to Ted and let him know what a bind he was putting her in. Russ agrees to do so, but he needs to know exactly what she needs: "Get me the details. I'll see Ted and see what I can do. I know they have some bugs to work out with the new software, but I don't imagine they're any happier about it than we are." Andrea, surprised, hadn't thought about it from that perspective and thanks Russ for his concern and help.

Other Communication Enhancers

Communication can also be encouraged by such actions as leaning forward, smiling, nodding, having direct eye contact, sticking to the subject under discussion, and paying full attention.

LIKELY REACTIONS AND CONSEQUENCES OF THE COMMUNICATION ATMOSPHERE

The importance of communication in the workplace cannot be overemphasized. Whether communication is closed or open will directly influence the amount of energy team members will expend.

Closed Communication

When communication-stoppers such as judging, superiority, and certainty abound in the workplace, the teams' likely reactions are disbelief and defensiveness. The likely undesirable consequences are that they will be reluctant to offer ideas, will wait for the manager to tell how they are going to do something, and won't own up to mistakes.

When communication-stoppers such as controlling and manipulating occur, team members are likely to become quiet and hesitate to ask questions. Some likely undesirable consequences are that the group will learn to distrust the manager's questions, will learn not to disagree, and will learn not to volunteer for anything.

When managers show indifference, such as continuing to write while others talk, changing the subject, or avoiding talking about the subject at hand, the likely reactions are for team members to be frustrated, annoyed, and impatient. Some likely undesirable consequences are they will learn to be indifferent themselves, will stop bringing up problems/issues to the manager, and will learn that their purpose is only to help the boss rather than vice versa.

Open Communication

When communication-encouragers such as description, equality, and openness abound in the workplace, the team's probable reaction is to be nondefensive. Likely positive consequences of such communication is that team members are willing to share ideas and to own up to difficulties and mistakes.

When managers encourage communication by asking for help, being up-front and honest, the team's likely reaction is to be positive, wanting to fulfill the manager's request and being willing to problem-solve through difficulties. As a result, the group will probably learn that the manager is willing to consider their needs, to negotiate, and to treat their problems seriously.

And when a manager shows empathy, the team is likely to react by being willing to give suggestions for solving problems and taking responsibility for taking initiative. Likely positive consequences are that they will learn to care and that the manager wants to help them solve their problems.

REVIEW OF COMMUNICATION DISCOURAGERS/ENCOURAGERS

Look at the following sets of behavior.

Discourages Communication	Encourages Communication
Judging	Description
Superiority	Equality
Certainty	Openness
Controlling	Problem-Orientation
Manipulation	Positive Intent
Indifference	Empathy

The preceding sets of behavior have been identified as leading to one of two situations:

> A work-unit climate of no trust where people tend not to share ideas, where people are reluctant to talk because it's punishing, or have quit talking because of learned apathy: "no use trying." The energy expended is extremely low, and there is limited or no shared responsibility.
>
> or
>
> A work-unit climate of trust where employees communicate solutions to problems and ideas for creating a better workplace. The energy level is extremely high, often synergistic, and responsibility for results (and failures) is shared by all members of the team and the team leader.

In summary, the word that describes when an employee is involved is *trust.* Trust is established by the way you encourage communication, two-way communication. If you consider the traditional approach to communication described at the beginning of this chapter, you should be sensing that here is another assumption you should think about questioning.

THE HIGH-COMMUNICATION TEAM IN ACTION

Consider your employees and where they are in their communication skills, their willingness to express ideas and opinions. Consider possible actions that might improve communication within your group.

Work groups with limited communication develop ideas individually (Lone Rangers) and feel little need to help other members of their group. The communication that does occur is often judgmental, controlling, or manipulative.

Work groups with average communication tend to have communication downward from the manager to members of the work unit. Work unit members provide limited feedback to each

Phase	Characteristics	Possible Actions
Team: (81 to 100)	• Communication among all group members is common. • Members are open to giving and receiving feedback. • Communication is open, empathetic, and solution-oriented.	• Encourage communication among all group members. • Reinforce members who provide and accept feedback. • Reinforce open, problem-solving communication.
Group: (61 to 80)	• Most work-related communication tends to be between leader and other members. • Members seldom provide constructive feedback for one another. • Communication among members is not oriented toward problem-solving.	• Encourage members to interact with other group members. • Offer constructive feedback to others and encourage group reviews of plans and results. • Emphasize the need for communication that is open, empathic, and solution-oriented.
Collection: (0 to 60)	• Members develop ideas without input from others. • Members feel little need to contribute to each other's tasks. • Communication is often judgmental, controlling, or manipulative.	• Facilitate group discussion of ideas and plans. • Encourage joint planning and implementation of projects. • Develop an awareness of how members discourage communication.

Figure 2 High communication—being willing to express ideas and opinions.

other, and their communication is usually not oriented toward problem-solving.

Work groups with high communication typically have open, empathic, solution-oriented communication. Group members talk openly with one another and with their manager and are open to giving and receiving feedback.

"The best way to predict the future is to create it."
—Peter Drucker

"Habit is habit, and not to be flung out of the window by any man, but coaxed downstairs a step at a time."
—Mark Twain

6

Focused on the Future—Is Change a Challenge?

Ask Yourself . . .

- Do your team members use the past as a guide for the future?
- Do they see change as an opportunity?
- Do they recognize the norms guiding their behavior?
- Is "can do" or "can't do" most evident?

An interesting experiment was performed using a fish tank divided in half by a clear glass partition. A Northern Pike was put in one half of the tank, and a number of small fish, normal food for the Northern Pike, were placed in the other half. The Northern Pike could see the small fish plainly, and it repeatedly crashed against the partition in an attempt to get at them. After a time, however, the Northern Pike gave up, having learned that it was no use. The experimenter then removed the partition. The small fish swam into the Northern's half of the tank, but the Pike made no effort to eat the fish. What the Northern Pike experienced in the past dictated how it reacted to the present, and it subsequently starved.

BEING STUCK

You've looked at some ways to stimulate the release of greater energy in your work unit. Just because you want to make changes to affect performance, however, does not mean the members of your work unit will go along with you. This chapter looks at what can have a greater influence over your employees' performance than you; at what can keep a group unable to grow, change, or perform as a team; and at how you can get a group willing to change, grow, and increase performance.

For starters, consider the situation of Valley View Industries, Inc. The company has initiated a "Team System" and is experiencing difficulty getting team meetings going. You are hired as a consultant to help with a specific group that is having trouble. Your first assignment is to sit in and observe the group.

> Russ's team is seated around a table looking bored and tired. Jerry methodically taps his pencil, staring into space. The silence is broken by Stan, "Boy, some proposal. What will our people say to this?"
>
> Linda adds, "And at the last minute, as usual. Good grief. Who put this thing together anyway? It's confusing. I can't follow any of it."
>
> Frank then chimes in with, "Nothing around here seems simple. You waste half your time trying to figure this stuff out."
>
> "Who's idea was this?" Stan asks.
>
> Jerry replies, "Our visionary colleagues over in marketing and sales."
>
> Stan nods, "That figures. Look at these functions. I'll never

get my people to agree to this. Who dreamed this stuff up? Why doesn't somebody tell them the facts of life?"

Linda shakes her head and says, "Nobody tells anybody anything around here. I don't even know where to start."

"Why start?" Stan asks. "When management takes a look at this, they'll panic and change everything anyway. They always do."

Linda voices her agreement, "Isn't it the truth? Why are we always in the middle of these crunches? It's all so futile."

And Jerry responds, "It comes with the territory as they say."

Think about this group's situation. They're obviously not getting much done, and are spending most of their time complaining. They are frustrated and dissatisfied. A key question is how would a group learn to be that way? It may start with one employee who thinks he or she is stuck and communicates that to the others. Over time, as the number of experiences grow and as the beliefs of the group members change, many of the group members may start behaving as if they were stuck. If enough of them believe and act stuck, they are, in fact, stuck—the familiar self-fulfilling prophecy.

To deal with a *stuck* situation, you need to understand how groups learn to behave as you just saw.

Two reasons teams become stuck are that *past experience* dictates what a group believes they can or cannot do and that the group has *commonly held beliefs and behavior patterns* that hinder high performance.

Past experiences and present beliefs can negatively affect group members' willingness to change, hindering the flow of productive energy in the work unit.

A common initial reaction to change is *resistance.* Past experience has taught that "It won't matter anyway," or "We tried that before, and it didn't work." This is often referred to as *learned apathy.*

LEARNED APATHY

Learned apathy is also referred to as "no commitment," "wheel spinning," "giving up," "going in circles," or "getting bogged down." The Northern Pike exhibited learned apathy. This phenomenon can be seen in most animal training. The elephant, for example, has been used as a beast of burden for centuries because of the ease with which it learns apathy. Training an elephant begins with chaining it to a very strong tree. The elephant struggles for a while, but ultimately gives up. Once the elephant's will is broken, the heavy chain can be removed. From that point on, the slightest restraint keeps the elephant in place. Even though it has the power to break out, when it attempts to walk away and meets resistance, it stops because it has learned, "Why bother; I'm not going anywhere anyway." It has learned not to resist. What it experienced in the past dictates how it reacts in the future. Both the elephant and the Northern Pike illustrate the common employee mind-set: "We tried that once and it didn't work."

Next consider learned apathy in a work setting. Go back to the meeting of Russ's group on pp. 92–93 and underline examples of learned apathy in that scenario. Next, imagine you are conducting the following meeting. As you read, underline the examples of learned apathy you notice.

The purpose of the meeting is to provide recommendations for changing a complex testing procedure. You explain that this team was chosen to work on the changes because they are closest to the problem.

> One team member states, "I think it's great that upper management finally realizes how inefficient the current process is." Another says, "How is it going to look if we suggest a change to the process that upper management supported for so long?" Someone else then asks, "So if they think this needs re-evaluating, where was it written that we ever had to follow it in the first place?" To which a colleague responds, "This is the way we've always done it—efficient or not!" "I'm so used to doing it this

way" adds another team member, "that it'll be tough to adjust to a new procedure."

As they continue discussing the issue, you acknowledge their expertise and talent and ask them to suggest some ideas for a new procedure. One person states, "We probably can come up with something, but the guys across the hall have their own ideas. We're not going to change their minds—no one has yet!"

After more discussion, all agree that if they can develop a new procedure and implement it, they would want it to be simple, making it easier to use. The objection now is, "Even if we keep it simple, no one will follow it because we don't have the authority to enforce it. We shouldn't even be bothering with this." Several team members agree.

As the meeting comes to a close, one team member who had remained silent during the meeting quietly points out, "If we could come up with something, it sure would reflect favorably on our department." To which another member adds, "Yes, but if we recommend something they like, it would be just like them to dump it back in our laps to make it happen. And who needs that?" Most of the group concurs.

Time runs out and the meeting ends without a decision. You promise to talk with your boss to see if the team should pursue the issue.

This example clearly illustrates several instances of learned apathy. The problem with learned apathy is that it can "take on a life of its own," meaning if people believe they are stuck, they are as good as stuck, and that belief begins feeding on itself. For example, if one member of a work unit declares that putting the budget on the computer won't work because it failed in the past, a new member who wasn't there at the time may hear the declaration and may think there is no point in pursuing the issue, even though he personally did not experience the situation. This belief ignores the fact that changes may have occurred that would make it possible to computerize the budget, as perhaps, for example, a better software package has been developed or a member of the team has taken a course in computerized accounting. Allowing the belief system to go unchallenged is a real danger to any team.

The most important thing is to recognize learned apathy for what it is, call it out, and challenge the team to find creative ways to get around it. Recognizing learned apathy is the first step to being able to do something about it.

GETTING UNSTUCK

A three-step approach can start the process of getting unstuck: (1) recognize, (2) describe, and (3) challenge.

Recognize. Before you can stop learned apathy, you need to be aware it is occurring. Listen for statements that keep a group stuck, e.g., "We tried that once and it didn't work." The underlying message here is that it won't work if they try again.

Describe. Once you observe learned apathy, describe to the group what is occurring. Do so as objectively as possible to avoid defensiveness. "I hear what you're saying. Based on our past experience with attempting to computerize the budget, it seems to be unlikely that it will work. It caused nothing but problems when we tried it before. But if we could get the budget computerized, it would save hundreds of hours and would eliminate the human errors that sometimes occur in calculations."

Challenge. Once the group is aware of what they have said and you have described the consequences, challenge them. Get them to think about why it didn't work or won't work and ask them to give you ideas on making it work or what is required for change. Point out the positive consequences that might result if a change were to occur. Ask "What if . . . ," and then fantasize about the possible outcomes.

Helping a team recognize and deal with their own learned apathy is a key to helping a group get unstuck. In addition, you need to look at the commonly held beliefs and patterns of behavior that may be keeping them from being a higher-performing team than they currently are. These commonly held beliefs or patterns of behavior are called *norms.*

NORMS

A norm is a system of shared values (what is important) and beliefs (how things work) that interact with people, organizational structures, and control systems to produce patterns of behavior (the way things are done around here).

A norm is to a group what a habit is to an individual.

Norms, like habits, have several positive aspects. They allow people to know what is expected, they help maintain order, they eliminate having to rethink every action, and they provide a sense of security.

On the other hand, norms also have some disadvantages or problems. They are resistant to change, they may get in the way of peak performance, and they may be engaged in unthinkingly. People may not understand why they are doing something a particular way; it's just the way it's done here.

Norms are all around us. Think for a minute about how people behave in an elevator: they get in, turn around, face the front, avoid eye contact with others, and seldom engage in conversation. Consider norms governing such behavior as handshaking, watching a sporting event, and dating.

One good example of norms is driving behavior. Ask yourself what you do when you approach an intersection and the light is red. You stop, right? That's the norm. It is also the law that you stop for a red light. Now ask yourself what is the norm for how fast people drive on the freeway? That may vary from city to city, but it is fair to say in most cases the norm is 60 to 65 mph. But the law is 55 mph. Here is a prime example of how the norm and the law may differ.

The same is true in a work environment. The company policy or the rules may not be what the norm really is. For example, it may be company policy that you take 15-minute breaks, but the norm may be to take 20-minute breaks. Or department policy may require that project status updates are turned in every Friday, but the norm is for them to trickle in the beginning of the following week.

Think about your own work situation. How many examples can you think of where the company or department policy is different from the norm? What are the expectations? How is one to communicate with upper management? Is there a dress code? Is it expected that people arrive at work on time? Limit breaks? Stay a certain number of hours? Attend the organization's Christmas party? Go to lunch with team members? The beliefs and behavior patterns in your work unit can be divided into three classifications:

1. Those that help the group be a high-performance team,
2. Those that hinder the group from being a high-performance team, and
3. Those that you, as leader, want the norms to be.

The third classification of norms, those that you desire, are future focused. And they are within reach. These may likely determine the degree of high performance attainable.

Whenever people come together, they eventually form a culture. This culture develops unwritten expectations and beliefs that strongly influence the behavior of the members of the culture. People can consciously design and shape the cultural norms rather than merely abide by them. And you, as a leader, can consciously help the group design and shape norms that encourage high performance. A norms identification exercise with your team can be extremely helpful. Because many norms operate at a subconscious level, team members are not aware of their powerful impact in shaping their behavior. The identification by your team of these norms allows you to do many things.

First, identifying *positive norms* allows you to make a conscious effort to reinforce those norms. Have you ever been in a situation where you used to do something valuable at work that isn't being done any more, and people ask each other, "Why don't we do that any more? That really helped." Often positive norms may "die on the vine" because of lack of support.

Second, identifying *negative norms* raises your awareness of how you get in your own way of performing as high as you would like. You can begin to do something about these norms. You may not be able to change every negative norm just because you raise your awareness, but failure to recognize them keeps you the victim of the norm.

Third, identifying *desired norms* allows you to take *ownership* for your own culture. This is a much healthier viewpoint than believing you are nothing more than a victim to the big organizational culture. Most teams have more control over their norms than they give themselves credit for. Taking responsibility for your own norms is a great way to demonstrate future focus.

John Zenger describes this responsibility for norms:

> Leaders also shape the culture and values that distinguish their organizations from all others. The philosophy and values of the Thomas Watsons, Sr. and Jr. shaped IBM. Ray D. Kroc's fetish for order, cleanliness, and quality spearheaded the success of McDonald's. Walt Disney's creative passion for technology and insistence on a clean park and well-trained employees created the legacy of Disneyland and Disney World. Lee Iacocca transformed Chrysler from a nearly defunct company into a serious competitor.

Once you have uncovered behavior patterns that need to be changed or identified norms you would like to exist in your work unit, how do you get your team members actually to change their behavior patterns?

One way is to sell them on your ideas. While sometimes selling may appear to work, in most instances it does not inspire much commitment or intention on the part of others. Without this commitment and intention, the result is likely to be mere compliance. An alternative to selling is *enrolling*.

ENROLLING

Remember the phrase "People do things for their reasons, not ours"? When enrolling others, you support them in supporting you, your intent, and your objectives based on *their* reasons, not yours. You discover their reasons for supporting you and help them recognize the benefits for them. You invite them to participate with you. And you *show* them whenever possible rather than simply telling them.

One process which can assist you in the enrolling process is called the *Balance of Consequences* (Frank Petrock).

THE BALANCE OF CONSEQUENCES

"What's in it for me?" People don't change just because they ought to or because you want them to or because the company would benefit if they did. The "Wish Style" of management won't bring about the desired changes. You may get frustrated with your team members because you are a self-starter. You exhibit high performance; why can't they?

When you expect a group to change, it is necessary to look at the consequences for doing so from the team members' perspectives. Although you want the change to occur, you must put yourself in their place to see the consequences for them. To understand why a group behaves in a particular way, ask, "What's in it for them to do or not to do the expected behavior?"

The Balance of Consequences is one way to answer that question. You begin by listing the desired behavior and the undesired behavior at the top of the sheet (see Figure 1).

This process works best with behavior patterns that are *specific, observable, and measurable.* For example, "arriving at work on time" is better than "exhibiting a positive attitude."

BALANCE OF CONSEQUENCES

DESCRIPTION OF THE DESIRED BEHAVIOR	DESCRIPTION OF THE UNDESIRED BEHAVIOR

NEGATIVE CONSEQUENCES	DIM	NEGATIVE CONSEQUENCES	DIM
POSITIVE CONSEQUENCES	**DIM**	**POSITIVE CONSEQUENCES**	**DIM**

DIM = Dimension (Personal or Organizational, Immediate or Delayed, Certain or a Gamble)

Figure 1 The balance of consequences.

Once you have stated the desired and undesired behavior, look at the situation as the "doer of the behavior" might.

Ask yourself:

- What are the positive consequences for doing the desired behavior?
- What are the negative consequences for doing the desired behavior?
- What are the positive consequences for doing the *un*desired behavior?
- What are the negative consequences for doing the *un*desired behavior?

Once you fill in the four quadrants, you are in a much better position to understand why someone is behaving as they are, and, therefore, are in a better position to know what to do to bring about a change in behavior.

To take a common example, consider the behavior of a three-year-old child who balks at going to bed on time. In this case the desired behavior is going to bed on time; the undesired behavior is not going to bed on time. As the child views it, the negative consequences for the desired behavior (going to bed on time) are that he misses out on the fun, he can't watch television, he has to stop playing, etc. The positive consequences for the desired behavior are minimal; in fact, the child probably doesn't see any. One positive consequence is that he will be more rested in the morning, but try to use that as a reason with the child.

And, as the child views it, the negative consequences for the undesired behavior (not going to bed on time) are that he may get spanked or he may get yelled at—not always, but sometimes. The positive consequences for the undesired behavior are that he gets attention, a glass of water, and often a story read to him. This is how the Balance of Consequences turns out for this behavior (Figure 2):

BALANCE OF CONSEQUENCES

DESCRIPTION OF THE DESIRED BEHAVIOR	DESCRIPTION OF THE UNDESIRED BEHAVIOR
Going to bed on time	Putting up a fuss at bedtime

NEGATIVE CONSEQUENCES	DIM	NEGATIVE CONSEQUENCES	DIM
Misses out on fun.	PIC	Parents spank him.	PDG
Can't watch TV.	PIC	Parents yell at him.	PIG
Has to stop playing.	PIC		
He's all alone.	PIC		
It's dark.	PIC		

POSITIVE CONSEQUENCES	DIM	POSITIVE CONSEQUENCES	DIM
More rested in the morning.	PDC	He gets attention.	PIC
		He gets a glass of water.	PIG
		He gets a story read to him.	PIG

DIM = Dimension (Personal or Organizational, Immediate or Delayed, Certain or a Gamble)

Figure 2 Balance of consequences in action.

This makes it understandable why the child doesn't go to bed on time.

How often is undesirable behavior rewarded? Think about the student who hates school, cuts up, and gets suspended. Is this punishment for the student or a reward?

Moreover, all too often, there are negative consequences for the desired behavior. Consider the person who consistently arrives at work early and is given the task of making the coffee. Or the person who turns in reports on time and is assigned additional work.

In addition to looking at negative and positive consequences, you should look at the types of consequences being provided and their strength.

Strength of Consequences

Consequences that are personal, immediate, and certain are stronger than those that are organizational, delayed, and gambled.

Personal consequences, as the name implies, affect an individual directly, for example, a pay raise. This is in contrast to organizational consequences, as, for example, the company makes a larger profit. People are more likely to work for their own raise than to help the company make a larger profit.

The more *immediate* the consequences, the stronger influence they tend to have on a person's behavior. A person will lie unprotected in the sun for hours, but will not put his or her hand into a fire. Gamblers receive immediate payoff when they win. Delayed consequences have a weaker influence. A person who exercises may feel the pain immediately; the payoff may be deferred for months. Likewise, bonuses paid yearly may be too delayed to provide much motivation. Daily contact by managers with their people giving them short, informal, and immediate feedback on their actions and progress provides immediate consequences as compared to relying solely on the annual performance review. These procedures are well outlined in *The One-Minute Manager* for one-to-one situations and can easily be adapted for one-to-group situations as well.

And the more *certain* the consequences, the stronger they are. If a person can identify a certain link between behavior and a consequence, that tends to be stronger than a situation where the person feels the consequence may or may not follow. A person who consistently speeds while driving and does not receive a ticket is likely to keep on speeding.

Think for a minute about how the Balance of Consequences might explain why smokers have such a difficult time stopping.

The undesired behavior (smoking) has numerous positive consequences, and most are personal, immediate, and certain: it's relaxing, tastes good, is sociable, and is comfortable (a habit). The negative consequences are personal, but they are distant and a gamble: cancer, emphysema, heart disease. In contrast, the positive consequences for the desired behavior (not smoking) are few, distant, and a gamble: save money and be healthier. The negative consequences for the desired behavior are immediate and certain: withdrawal pains, irritability, weight gain, and stress. (See Figure 3.)

If you return to the example of the child who does not want to go to bed on time and look at the types of consequences occurring, you'll notice that a similar situation exists. Likewise, the balances of consequences helps to explain why an assembly line worker has little incentive to offer productivity improvement ideas that could result in the loss of his or her job or even a job of a peer.

Or consider the employee who leaves important work unfinished on her desk to attend a meeting, but the meeting doesn't start on time. She begins coming to meetings late and not only gets more of her work done, but also receives much attention from others when she arrives at the meeting in progress. She is likely to continue arriving late.

BALANCE OF CONSEQUENCES

DESCRIPTION OF THE DESIRED BEHAVIOR	DESCRIPTION OF THE UNDESIRED BEHAVIOR
NOT smoking	Smoking

NEGATIVE CONSEQUENCES	DIM	NEGATIVE CONSEQUENCES	DIM
Withdrawal pains	PIC	Cancer, emphysema, hear disease	PDG
Irritable	PIC	Expensive	PIC
Weight gain	PDG	People may shun you	PIG
Stress	PIC	Smelly	PIC

POSITIVE CONSEQUENCES	DIM	POSITIVE CONSEQUENCES	DIM
Healthier	PDC	Relaxing	PIC
Save $	PIC	Tastes good	PIC
Smell better	PIC	Sociable	PIC
		Comfortable (habit)	PIC

DIM = Dimension (Personal or Organizational, Immediate or Delayed, Certain or a Gamble)

Figure 3 Balance of consequences in action.

Options for Changing Consequences

You have four options for changing consequences: 1) create more positive consequences for the desired behavior, 2) remove negative consequences for the desired behavior, 3) remove the positive consequences for the undesired behavior, and 4) increase the negative consequences for the undesired behavior. In the case of the assembly line worker, you might offer financial incentives for productivity-improving ideas and guarantee employment. You can give positive recognition for even small ideas.

In the case of the employee who habitually arrives late for meetings, you might practice any of the following four options.

1. Discuss with the employee additional responsibilities, improved performance ratings, or additional recognition she will be given if she arrives at meetings on time.
2. Assure her that the meeting will begin and finish on time, thus allowing her to return to the other tasks that obviously now are preventing her from attending the entire meeting.
3. If her motive for arriving late is to receive recognition from the remainder of the group, assure her that she will receive greater recognition within the group if she arrives on time.
4. Explain to her that if she does not arrive on time, she will no longer be asked to attend meetings (unless she would view this as positive). As a result, she will not have information available to the rest of the group, resulting in a decrease in her value to the group and her ability to perform her job.

If you expect people to change, they need to feel there is something in it for them to do so. The Balance of Consequences helps you understand the existing consequences and provides a strategy to change the consequences to favor the desired behavior.

Phase	Characteristics	Possible Actions
Team: (81 to 100)	• Members focus on long-term success, while considering short-term needs. • Members use innovative and creative approaches to solving problems. • Change is perceived as providing opportunities to explore new ideas or strategies.	• Encourage attempts to balance short-term and long-term needs. • Support new approaches to solving problems. • Reinforce positive attitudes toward change.
Group: (61 to 80)	• Members consider future needs, but review options in terms of short-term success. • Members are aware of group norms that prevent change. • Consequences for change are unclear.	• Help members consider long-term as well as short-term rewards. • Encourage members to challenge and alter norms that prevent change. • Facilitate discussions to analyze the advantages and disadvantages of change.
Collection: (0 to 60)	• Members focus on reviewing past problems or successes as a guide for decision-making. • Members are unaware of how group norms prevent experimentation. • Change is seen as a threat.	• Encourage members to anticipate future needs and identify new opportunities. • Facilitate discussions to identify group norms that prevent experimentation. • Help members minimize the risks associated with change by initially taking small steps.

Figure 4 Future focus—seeing change as an opportunity for growth.

A FUTURE-FOCUSED TEAM IN ACTION

Take a few minutes to see how future focused your team is now. (Figure 4). Teams with low performance tend to focus on past problems rather than on future opportunities. Those with average performance accept change, but with apprehension. They prefer the status quo rather than growth and change. Those with high performance look forward to change, seeing it as a challenge and an opportunity to be innovative.

A company's success is inversely proportional to the number of meetings it holds.

A meeting is an event where minutes are kept and hours are lost.

7

Focused on Task: Do Your Meetings Produce Results?

Ask Yourself . . .

- Do members come to meetings prepared?
- Do members participate in meetings?
- Do meetings stay on track?

Two groups were holding meetings in conference rooms right beside each other. Group A was vocal, energetic, and obviously having fun. Group B, in contrast, was subdued. The leader had the urge to hold a mirror under some of the participants' noses to check for breathing. No bumps (heads dropping on the table) were heard from Group A, but Group B's bump level was high. During a break, a participant from Group B cornered the leader of his group and said, "I sure wish I was in their group (Group A). Sounds like they're having fun."

"Let me ask you a question," the leader said. "How many of you are there?"

"Seventeen," the participant responded.

"And how many of me?" the leader queried.

"One."

"Well," Leader B stated, "if you want to have fun, have fun. It's your group."

The members of this group are like most people. They have learned that if something is going to happen in a meeting, it is because the leader makes it happen. Therefore, how you conduct meetings is a very important part of creating a high-performance team.

THE BIG PICTURE

One of the themes of this book is that teamwork depends on people having tasks that are interdependent. Another theme is that you can often be more efficient managing one-to-group than one-to-one, in which case meetings will be probably be frequent. Yet, as attested to by the opening quotes to this chapter, meetings are often regarded as a waste of time—sometimes rightfully so. We will look at some of the reasons for ineffective meetings in a moment, but first, let us place meetings in their correct perspective.

Just as a quarterback calls his players together after almost every play, you, as a leader, will call your team together to capitalize on the advantages of the one-to-group skills you are developing. Use those skills during the meetings. You will want to be a participative leader, to share responsibility for the meeting with the members of the group, to keep the participants aware of their overall purpose or unique contribution, to encourage open communication, and to keep from getting stuck.

The preceding factors are attributes of a high-performance team. When they are present, team members give not only time, but energy. Human energy produces best results when it is *focused*. Focused energy is illustrated in Figure 1.

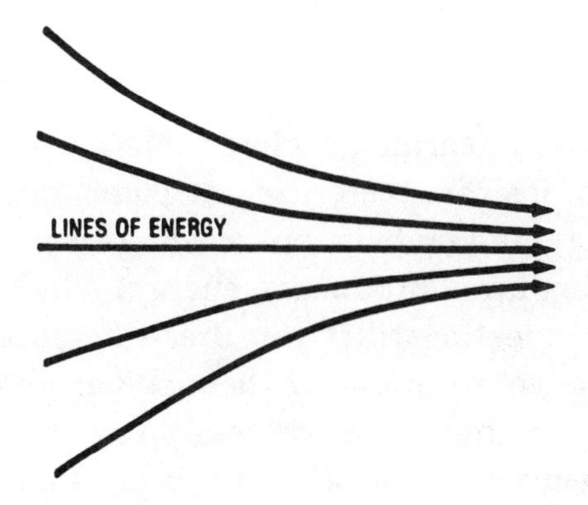

Figure 1 Focused energy.

When energy is focused, people feel as if they are getting somewhere.

Sometimes, however, situations arise when energy is unfocused, people feel frustrated, unproductive, as though they were wasting their time and energy. And, without a focus, they usually are. Unfocused energy is represented in the diagram in Figure 2.

What is the one situation where you interact with your work unit as a group where it seems most difficult to keep

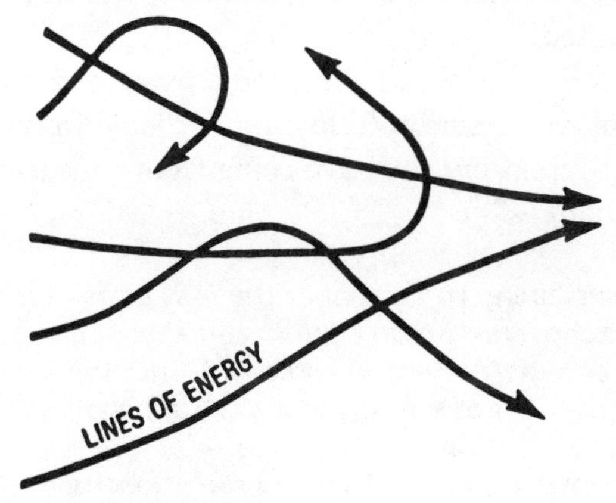

Figure 2 Unfocused energy.

everyone's energy focused on the task at hand? If you're like the vast majority of managers, *meetings* comes immediately to mind.

When Wilson Learning explored what depletes human energy, common answers were: lack of communication, conflict between people, and no help, but meetings were most often included as taking away productive energy. Why? Take a minute to think about meetings that you dread because they are unproductive. We've all attended them. What people behaviors squelched the meeting's effectiveness?

You probably thought of such things as members' getting off the topic, wanting to rehash the last meeting, becoming angry, sermonizing, having hidden agendas, not being prepared, spending too much time on low priorities, carrying on side conversations and not attending to the person who has the floor, and exhibiting any of the communication inhibitors discussed in Chapter Five.

What other factors related to meetings tend to frustrate you? How about meetings that don't start on time? Those that have no clear agenda? Those that have people there who don't need to be and others not there who should be? Those that don't end on time? Those that take place in uncomfortable surroundings? How do you feel after attending a meeting that was a complete waste of time? Probably frustrated, tense, angry, maybe even exhausted.

You can tell a lot about the productivity of a meeting by listening to the conversation following it. Listen in on members of Melonie's group after they have come from a meeting dealing with design changes:

> Tom is complaining to Ted about the way Stan kept rattling on about switchovers, "I didn't think he'd ever shut up."
>
> Ted agrees and voices additional irritation with Fred, "If he mentions the problems his group is having with the software program one more time . . . I swear—."
>
> He's interrupted by Tom's observation that the meeting was supposed to be a short status report, but for some it was a

regular laundry list of crying towels. He asks Tom why Melonie didn't cut them off.

Tom doesn't know, but warns, "She'd better start though, unless she wants these reports to turn into two hour meetings."

Tom and Ted aren't the only team members complaining. Stan and Linda are griping too. Linda can't believe Harold's attitude at the meeting, "If you talk about something he's not interested in, he accuses you of making your status reports too long."

Stan asks Linda why she didn't say something, and she replies, "Are you kidding? It's not up to me to bring that up. That's Melonie's job."

Meanwhile, Fred shows up in Melonie's office and wants to talk to her. He's concerned about how difficult it's going to be for his people to update the software system once it's installed.

Melonie says she wishes he'd shared that concern at the meeting and asks why he didn't. His response: "I don't know. It didn't seem like the right place to bring it up."

Melonie shakes her head and replies, "I wish you had brought it up. The whole purpose of those meetings is to share information and concerns. That meeting is as much yours as it is anybody elses."

Without having attended this meeting, you know that it was not productive. Turn your attention now to meetings that *are* productive. What's different about them?

WELL-RUN MEETINGS

Meetings are the primary setting where one-to-group management skills are exercised and the place where these skills can have the greatest impact on the performance of the team. The way you and the members of your work unit behave when you come together in meetings is an important factor in creating a high-performance team.

Take a minute and recall a meeting that you have attended which you would describe as well run. What were the characteristics of this meeting? Most well-run meetings have a clear sense of purpose, with everyone's participating, but with no one allowed to go off on tangents, and they last no longer than necessary.

Since these are all familiar characteristics, why aren't there more well-run meetings? One way to answer this question is to reflect on the gripes of Melonie's group in the preceding scenario. They left the meeting frustrated and disgusted and spent their energy griping and complaining. They probably spent their energy during the meeting thinking negatively and blaming the leader for the ineffectiveness of the meeting. For a team to increase its focus on task needs, everyone on the team needs to understand and agree to an important norm.

Well-run meetings are the responsibility of *both* the leader and the members of the team.

Unfortunately, in most cases, the mentality in meetings is that it is the leader's meeting. It's important for task focus that team members also feel a sense of responsibility for what happens in meetings.

As a leader, you can increase your team's task focus in several ways:

- Making sure the team knows the purpose of the meeting, how that purpose will be achieved, and what significance it has for the team.
- Creating an environment in which people are willing to participate.
- Dealing effectively with team members when they go off task.
- Establishing positive expectations for team-member behavior.

Appendix A contains many useful suggestions to help you establish a positive meeting context. Such things as agendas, having the audio-visual equipment checked out, and the like are certainly important for well-run meetings. Even more important, however, is your behavior during a meeting.

STARTING AN EFFECTIVE MEETING

It's important to focus on task at the start of a meeting. Have you ever been in a meeting that you could tell in the first five minutes was going to be a bad one? Think about what you said to yourself. Was it something like "Oh no, not another one of these," "Why do I have to be here?" "Where is this leading?" or "This is going to be a waste of time"?

People typically walk into a meeting with three key questions. How these questions get answered has a lot to do with whether they choose to focus a lot or a little energy to the meeting. These questions are "Why am I here?" "What are we going to do?" and "What's in it for me?"

Since these are questions people have anyway, why not take them into account as part of your meeting introduction using a three-step model, *purpose/process/payoff.*

PURPOSE/PROCESS/PAYOFF

An easy, effective way to begin a meeting takes the planning you did for the meeting and puts it to work right up front. The participants learn why they are there, what direction they are headed, and what to expect when they get there.

Purpose. This answers the question "Why am I here?" Share the objective of the meeting and, when appropriate, how it fits into the team's common purpose. Stating the purpose answers questions the team members might have such as: Why are we here? Why am I here? What do I offer? What are we trying to accomplish? What is our goal?

Process. This answers the question "What are we going to do?" Tell them the process they will follow. Briefly cover the agenda items with them and tantalize them with what they can expect to experience. Remind them to be flexible. Stating the process answers questions team members might have such as: What's the agenda? How will we proceed? What activities will we be doing? What's the road map—what steps will we follow? How long will this last? What's expected of me? Am I supposed to offer suggestions? What can I expect from the leader? How will what I offer be used?

Payoff. This answers the question "What's in it for me?" Share how the team will benefit from the meeting. This step could include either how the company may benefit, or particularly how the *members of the team* will benefit, or both. Remember that personal consequences are much stronger than organizational consequences as you describe the payoff of the meeting. Stating the payoff answers questions such as: Why bother? Who will benefit from this? What's in it for me? How can I really benefit? How will what we do be put into effect?

Purpose/process/payoff is an easy, effective way to start any meeting. It allows the participants to know why they are there, what road they are going to follow, and what to expect when they get there.

To see the purpose/process/payoff model in action, picture the following:

> Melonie's team is gathered for another meeting. She begins the meeting on time with, "I know you're all busy, so let's get started. I wanted to get together today to let you know about some key configuration changes in the Tremain project."
>
> Fred asks how many changes there are, and Melonie responds, "Before I get into answering specific questions, let me give you an overall plan of how we'll proceed at this meeting.

First I'd like to give you a brief overview of the major changes. I'll ask you to hold your thoughts at that point. Then we'll go back and look at each change in more detail. Then I'd like to hear any questions or comments you might have. It's important that we completely understand each of these changes. After that I want you to have an opportunity to express your concerns and comments."

The team members express enthusiastic interest in what changes have been made as Melonie continues, "I think you'll find these changes in the overall design will make implementation easier, and that will make for a better product when it's finished. Any questions before we go on? (A chorus of "no's.")

The meeting went smoothly and was productive because the manager defined the purpose: ". . . let me know about some key configuration changes on the Tremaine project." She described the process: ". . . quickly give you an overview of the major changes, and then we'll go back and look at each one in more detail. At that point I'd like to hear questions and comments." And she described the payoff: ". . . We can implement the changes without problems . . . really help the overall design, and it'll be a better product."

Meetings are like meeting a person for the first time; first impressions are everything. Using purpose/process/payoff can help you establish a positive first impression of your meetings. The next question is how to keep the meeting going in a positive way after it gets started.

ASSUMPTIONS ABOUT MEETING PARTICIPANTS

The assumptions of a leader have a great deal to do with the behavior exhibited in a meeting and, consequently, with the behavior of the members of the meeting. Consider the following assumptions a meeting leader may make, the verbal form they may take, and how the statements may affect the behavior of people in a meeting.

Assumption	Verbal Expression
They won't understand the details.	"Without going into too much detail—."
Don't spend time explaining; they'll just get into other issues you don't want to deal with.	"Without going into the whys, the changes are really basic."
It is pretty simple; they shouldn't have a lot of questions.	"Once you hear the changes, you shouldn't have any questions."
They won't have any comments; they never have anything of value.	"If no one has any comments, I'll move on to the next item."

What are the likely effects of such assumptions on the group leader's behavior? The leader will probably fail to communicate enough detail, will appear evasive, and will give little opportunity for participation.

The effect of these negative assumptions on the attitudes and behavior of team members is that they are likely to feel negative and choose not to participate.

Other common negative assumptions about meeting participants include the following: they always go off on tangents; they only come to meetings to get time off from work; they view meetings as a waste of time; I already know what they're going to say; and they don't understand the real problems.

Self-Fulfilling Prophecies

Negative expectations tend to become self-fulfilling prophecies. In other words—how you expect things to turn out has a profound effect on the actual outcome of events. This is true because your expectations will, to a large extent, determine how you choose to behave in a given situation. So, what does this say to you about generating participation in a meeting?

It's important that you are aware of your negative assumptions and, more importantly, to have positive assumptions going into a meeting. If you enter a meeting with positive expectations, you can act in such a way that team members are encouraged to participate more easily. In addition, you can do other things to generate participation.

GENERATING PARTICIPATION

- Ask open-ended questions.
- Call on people directly.
- Ask people to come prepared.
- Reinforce on-purpose statements.
- Ask members of the group to acknowledge each other.
- Use prompts: verbal and nonverbal.
- Use appropriate silence—wait for answers.
- Redirect questions asked of you to other members of the team (sometimes back to the one who asked).
- Use ice breakers and warm-up exercises.
- Avoid win/lose situations.
- Summarize and restate key comments.
- Self-disclose—share personal examples.
- Write key statements on flipchart and post.
- Make eye contact.
- Move close to the person you want to reinforce.
- Use humor.
- Stay open to the viewpoints of others.
- Describe to the group what you see occurring.

Once you've generated participation, you need to concentrate on keeping the team focused on their agenda.

KEEPING THE TEAM ON TASK

Off-task behavior is behavior that doesn't contribute to helping the team achieve the task at hand. Such behavior includes things like jumping ahead in the agenda, going off on tangents, monopolizing the discussion, or intimidating others. The way a leader handles these situations is an important factor in keeping meetings productive. The following behaviors can keep a group on task:

- Restate specific objectives of the meeting.
- Ask task-related questions.
- Express your feelings about staying on task.
- Ignore off-task remarks—don't reinforce.
- Reinforce on-task remarks.
- Make summarizing statements when someone starts to wander, then ask someone else to comment.
- Check with the group to see if there is a consensus that the subject is on task.
- Require the group to deal in specific areas.
- Ask a closed-ended question (requires a yes or no response) to the off-task person, and redirect an open-ended question (requires more information) to someone else.
- Tactfully ask the person to stop and allow others to discuss the topic at hand.
- At the very start of the session, ensure that everyone knows they will have a chance to speak.
- Use a hand gesture to indicate to the person to hold on.
- Focus attention on the person who is off task so that other group members help the person get back on track.
- Ask the person to help relate his/her statement to the task at hand.
- Write information on the easel or chalkboard so people can see the kinds of ideas that are being expressed.

It's important to be in touch with the behavior patterns that keep a group on task and how well you can use these patterns. As you think about how to do this, consider who taught team members to be good meeting participants. In most cases, managers have not put a lot of energy into teaching team members how to be good meeting participants. They just expect them to learn as they go.

If well-run meetings are the responsibility of both the leader and the members of the team, leaders can do a lot to help the team members get clear on what is expected of them. What behavior should a participant exhibit in an ideal meeting? The answer is, of course, the same behavior an effective meeting leader should exhibit. Most importantly, all team members should realize they share responsibility for the meeting and should come prepared, arrive on time, participate, stay focused, listen to others' views, and commit to accomplishing the purpose of the meeting.

IN SUMMARY

Purpose/process/payoff is an important way to get a meeting off to a good start and to help people be focused on task. You need to be aware of the expectations/assumptions you have about team members' willingness and ability to participate in meetings and to be aware of effective leader behavior for keeping your team on task. Finally, you need to inform team members of what is expected of them in terms of effective meeting behavior.

A TASK-FOCUSED TEAM IN ACTION

Spend a few minutes considering how task focused your team is now (Figure 3). Teams with low performance on this attribute view meetings as a waste of time; people don't come to meetings prepared; and little energy is directed toward the meeting's purpose.

Phase	Characteristics	Possible Actions
Team: (81 to 100)	• Meetings usually accomplish preestablished objectives.	• Take time to acknowledge group accomplishments.
	• Members participate in reaching the goals of the meeting.	• Reinforce members who keep the group focused on results.
	• Members are prepared for meetings.	• Continue to clarify expectations and reinforce contributions.
Group: (61 to 80)	• Meetings sometimes accomplish objectives.	• Make sure objectives are realistic and that members agree to them.
	• Meetings seem to shift focus.	• Encourage members to share responsibility for progress during meetings.
	• Members are sometimes prepared for meetings.	• Clarify expectations and reinforce preparation.
Collection: (0 to 60)	• Objectives for meetings are unclear.	• Prepare an agenda and focus on specific objectives.
	• Members allow the meeting to move away from the focus.	• Establish ground rules to help meetings progress efficiently.
	• Members come unprepared for meetings.	• Clarify purpose and roles prior to meetings.

Figure 3 Task focus—keeping meetings focused on results.

Teams with average performance on this attribute feel little of concrete value is accomplished during meetings. Their meetings are not focused and tend to be critical and judgmental.

In contrast, teams who are outstanding on this attribute have meetings with clear purpose. Most members come prepared, and there is a general belief that meetings are important.

"Imagination is more important than knowledge. For knowledge is limited, whereas imagination embraces the entire world."

—Albert Einstein

"Anyone who can spell a word only one way is an idiot."

—W. C. Fields

8

Creative Talents: Who's Got an Idea?

Ask Yourself . . .

- Do your team members balance idea generation and idea evaluation?
- Is creativity, as well as immediate results, rewarded?
- Do team members rely on patterns as they approach solutions to problems?
- Does your team think innovatively?

A man once spent over an hour trying to rescue his little boy's pet frog from the bottom of a narrow shaft in their back yard. He tried a long stick, then a rope with a loop at the end, then an open-ended can on a string, but nothing worked. Finally he gave up and went in the house to watch a football game.

Minutes later his five-year-old son appeared, with his frog. The boy had flooded the shaft with a garden hose and floated the frog to the surface.

Dudley Lynch, in *You're Smarter Than You Think,* states that:

> In the wild kingdom of their imagination, children are forever coming up with creative solutions. Unlike adults, children have an open pipeline to the seat of creativity: the right hemisphere of the brain. But when they start school, the "left brain"—the seat of logic—begins falling victim to the fears, rules, obligations and concerns of the adult world and, before long, imagination is in retreat. What sets the creative person off from the rest of us is that he or she has somehow managed to hold onto a childlike curiosity and an unbounded sense of creative possibility.

He goes on to note that over the past 15 to 20 years social scientists have studied the power of creative thinking and have come to believe that: ". . . creativity is far more common than previously thought. In fact, most researchers claim there is a spark of genius in each of us, waiting to be freed."

BARRIERS TO CREATIVITY

Since people are naturally creative, the intent of this chapter is not to teach you to be creative, but rather to help you understand what often gets in the way of creativity and how to overcome those barriers. Two key areas prevent creativity from occurring:

1. How you limit your own thinking and
2. How members of a group limit one another's participation.

Limit Thinking	**Limit Participation**
Habits	Norms and rules
Self-criticism	Criticism of others
Emotions	Intimidation
Patterns of thinking	Combining idea generation with idea evaluation

Individuals frequently limit their own creativity by allowing themselves to "get stuck," to rely on what has worked in the past and to exhibit learned apathy. They may also lack confidence in their own creative talents. Even Aldous Huxley doubted his abilities in the creative area: "I am and, for as long as I can remember, have always been a poor visualizer. Words, even the pregnant words of poets, do not evoke pictures in my mind" (*The Brain: Mystery of Matter and Mind,* p. 69). Have you ever said to yourself that you just weren't creative? In addition to self-criticism, individuals may limit their own creativity by becoming emotionally involved with the task or by confining their thinking to a set pattern.

Groups, too, frequently limit their creativity. They get stuck through learned apathy. They impose barriers to open communication by criticizing others' ideas and suggestions. They lack confidence as a group. And they are unable to generate alternative approaches without judging them. In effect, they throw an idea out on the table and then proceed to stab it to death. This chapter focuses on identifying how individuals and groups limit their creative talents and on ways to remove these barriers and allow creative synergy to occur. You can never tell which way the train went by looking at the track.

Functional Fixation

To begin looking at how creativity is sometimes limited, consider how you limit your own thinking. Often it is limited by a phenomenon called *functional fixation,* that is, thinking about what you can do with something. To demonstrate this phenomenon to yourself, imagine you have been given the task to come up with as many uses for a wire coat hanger as you can. Take a few minutes to think about it.

As you thought about the uses for a coat hanger, you probably experienced functional fixation, concentrating on what coat hangers are normally used for and not being able to generate many new uses. Functional fixation allows the form, shape, and size of something to hinder how you think about it.

What if instead you had been told you had a warehouse of wire? Would it have been easier to think of uses for the wire from which the hanger was made? Probably so. But there's a good chance you still will limit your creativity if you focus on the wire. You can break this pattern by approaching the issue differently.

Ask what you *can't* do with something rather than what you can do with it.

What can't you do with a coat hanger? You can't eat it, right? So, related to that, what *can* you do? Think about it. You might make a fork, a stick to cook with, a barbecue grill, chopsticks, etc. What else can't you do with a wire coat hanger? You can't listen to it. Related to listening, what can you make? How about an antenna, a guitar string, a tuning fork, a speaker. You can't fly a coat hanger, but you could make it into a spear, a boomerang, or the core for a model airplane.

Asking what you can't do with something helps you get outside the fixation of what you commonly can do with it. This typically will trigger many ideas you would not have considered. It also illustrates what happens when you get caught in a pattern.

Patterns prevent you from making obvious connections. A classic example of breaking a pattern of thinking is Jack Nicklaus's solution to the challenge of making a small golf course in the Cayman Islands. While everyone else focused on how to design the course, Nicklaus changed the ball so that it wouldn't travel as far when it was hit.

It is essential to break patterns to make novel and useful new connections. This is, in fact, one definition of creativity.

Creativity is the process of breaking *old* connections and making useful *new* connections.

Patterns that Limit Thinking

Breaking connections or patterns is difficult. The mind gets locked into patterns very quickly. For example, consider the following cheer: "Rah, rah ree. Kick 'em in the knee. Rah, rah, rass. Kick 'em in the other knee." The humor comes from the unexpected last line.

Recall the discussion on being stuck. This is often the result of thinking there's only one way to do a thing: "This is how we've always done it." Following is a list of common patterns of thinking which often limit creative thinking.

- If it isn't broken, don't fix it (limited vision).
- I must get this right the first time (no room for error).
- It'll keep until tomorrow (procrastination).
- Better safe than sorry (no room for experimentation).
- If only . . . (wishful thinking).
- I'm not creative enough (self-doubt).
- There's only one way to do this (no room for innovation).
- This is good enough (selling short).
- I'm not the kind of person who . . . (limited role).
- I am the kind of person who . . . (limited role).

Such patterns of thinking may be useful sometimes, but more often than not they get in the way of creativity. A useful way to break such patterns is to think about why the pattern is useful and helpful. For example, when is the pattern, "If it isn't broken, don't fix it," useful? When conditions haven't changed and a certain approach is still functional, or when there are other higher priorities and what's working doesn't warrant changing now. After you think about when a pattern of thinking is helpful, you can turn your attention to thinking about the conditions under which the pattern isn't useful. This puts you in a position to make a conscious decision about thinking differently about the situation. You might, for example, say, "Just because it's not broken yet doesn't mean it will be successful forever. Now is a good time to start thinking about how to improve it."

As you look at patterns of thinking and how they affect creativity, it may be helpful to look at some research on how the brain processes information.

Right/Left-Brain Thinking

Twenty-five centuries ago Hippocrates startled the world by contending that thought and emotion came from the brain, not the heart. He also noted that a wound on the left side of the head affected the function of only the right side of the body.

Twenty-five years ago another physician, Roger Sperry, and his students, in significant left-right brain research, determined that each side of the brain has its own thoughts and memories and processes information differently. The left side (in a right-handed person) processes language—reading, writing, and speaking. It is the logical part of our thinking. The right side processes images. It is visual and sensory. That is, the verbal brain we talk to, the left side, sees and feels with the right side, and the *corpus callosum* is the cable connecting the communication.

Dr. Sperry and his students experimented with people whose corpus callosum was severed and found that when these people were flashed the letters, de-on the left brain identified the word as "noon," the right brain as the word "deed." When flashed the letters sh-dy, the left brain 90 percent of the time selected a lady picture, the right brain chose a shoe picture. In 1981 Roger Sperry was awarded the Nobel Prize in medicine for his remarkable findings. His breakthrough clearly demonstrated the division of labor between the sides of the brain and the critical role of the corpus callosum. (Damage to the corpus callosum is now considered by some to be the cause of certain forms of dyslexia.)

Current brain research also indicates differences in the way each hemisphere of our brain processes information. Generally, the right hemisphere processes *spatial* information, while the left hemisphere processes *linear* information. Right-brain thinking is more holistic, intuitive, nonrational, concrete, nontemporal, and nonverbal. Left-brain thinking is more segmented, logical, rational, symbolic, temporal, and verbal.

A federally funded project in the Minneapolis Public Schools directed by Mary Oberg has generated the following chart to summarize their review of the recent research on left-right brain functioning:

Left Hemisphere	**Right Hemisphere**
small logical linear steps	looks at the whole situation at once (holistic, gestalt)
successive	simultaneous
phonetic reader	whole word reader
grammatical correctness	figurative style, metaphoric
knows names	recognizes faces
knows right/wrong, black/white	sees the "grays"
words	visual images
math	the arts
writing	music
reading	sees in 3D—detects patterns
controls right side	controls left side
reasoning	imagination
day thinking	day dreaming
literal meaning	tone of voice, body language
conscious	unconscious, preconscious
thinker	sensor
lawyer	sculptor
research of Skinner	research of Freud

Immanuel Kant	da Vinci
Aldous Huxley	Michelangelo
verbal coach, self 1	silent player, self 2
Western thought	Eastern thought
objective	subjective
scientific skills	insight
intellectual	sensuous
logical	"feel for it"
abstract	concrete
convergent	divergent
vertical thinking	lateral thinking
verifies ideas	generates ideas
digital	spatial
rational	nonrational
sequential	nonsequential

The issue is not which mode is more creative. The western world and its educational system tend to use—and are better at—the left-brain approach to problem solving, preferring a rational, logical, analytical approach. What is needed, however, is a "whole brain" approach, using the right brain more effectively in the creative process. As noted by Carl Sagan:

> There is no way to tell whether the patterns extracted by the right hemisphere are real or imagined without subjecting them to the left hemisphere scrutiny. On the other hand, mere critical thinking, without creative and intuitive insights, without the search for new patterns, is sterile and doomed. To solve complex problems in changing circumstances requires the activity of both cerebral hemispheres: the path to the future lies through the corpus callosum (Sally Spring and George Deutsch, *Left Brain/Right Brain* p.192).

Now that you have looked at some patterns that limit thinking and how use of both hemispheres of the brain is needed for optimal creativity, look at the second area of limitation—barriers that limit how group members participate with each other.

Barriers that Limit Participation

To begin with, picture yourself as part of Melonie's team listening to Fred's solution to a design change problem.

> Stan suggests that the solution is a little radical and that the powers that be will want to go along with their regular format, the way it's always been done.
>
> Linda agrees, saying, "It's a good idea, but we'd better move cautiously. In the long run, it might be more trouble than it's worth."
>
> Harold, too, likes the idea and thinks it would work, but questions whether they have the authority. Linda then reminds them that they had tried something similar before and gotten into all kinds of trouble.
>
> At this point Melonie interjects, "I really don't think that's what the company has in mind," and Fred suggests, "Maybe we're too close. Why don't we bring Rollins in from manufacturing to play devil's advocate?"
>
> Melonie strenuously objects to the suggestion, "That's just asking for trouble. We can do our own work here. We don't need Rollins."
>
> Linda then repeats her support for the idea, but says she thinks they would be taking on more than they can handle. Fred's response? "Oh well, it was just an idea."

You can probably readily identify with this situation. Most people have, at least once in their lives, presented an idea and received a series of reasons why the idea won't work.

Sometimes our work unit norms become the patterns which act as barriers to creativity. Often these norms are beliefs and attitudes about what can and cannot be done. When they are expressed, they sound like *killer phrases.*

Killer Phrases

Killer phrases are the negative comments made in response to an idea. They are judgments and criticism that stifle creativity. They are often the result of learned apathy. Following are some examples of such killer phrases:

"That's too radical."

"It's contrary to policy."

"We must follow the rules."

"That's not our area."

"I'm not creative."

"Won't fit within deadline."

"We'll never get help."

"That's too much hassle."

"It just won't work."

"It worked before."

"Too obvious."

"Be practical."

"Don't be frivolous."

"Costs too much."

"We've never done it that way before."

"We must have a total solution."

"Be realistic."

"Get serious."

These killer phrases can be either internal self-talk or external communication. Either way, they form a major barrier to creativity. Recall the earlier discussion of communication barriers: certainty, judging, etc.

What can be done about them? The key to handling killer phrases is to recognize them, describe to the group what you see occurring, and to challenge the basis on which the statements are being made. If you notice killer phrases, no matter who is actually saying them—you or a member of your group—use the Recognize-Describe-Challenge process you learned to deal with learned apathy.

Recognize. The first step in handling killer phrases—recognizing them—is a function of the group's awareness and commitment to creativity and high performance. Your job as leader is to support and reaffirm this commitment and to point out errors as they occur. Take a moment to notice any killer phrases that occur and to ask yourself if this is helping or hindering your purpose.

Describe. Describe what you hear occurring. Remember to do so objectively to avoid defensiveness by the person using the phrase.

Challenge. Ask the group to remain open to ideas and challenge them to stay creative, rather than stopping ideas from developing.

In addition to watching for killer phrases, you should be aware of another way in which participation is limited.

Diverge/Converge

Frequently when people are asked to generate alternatives, they immediately start looking for the best idea. Instead of generating as many ideas as possible without discussion and later evaluating the ideas, they start discussing the ideas too soon in the process.

To *diverge* means to open up or explode out, to look for as many options as possible. In contrast, to *converge* is to bring back together and refine ideas, or select the best options. These two contrasting activities are illustrated in Figure 1.

Obviously both diverging and converging play a major role in the creative process. The problem is that participation is limited if you try to do them both at the same time. To be effective in the creative process, you need to separate these two functions. However, all too often, just the opposite occurs. Once a good idea is brought up, people stop looking for other possible alternatives and begin discussing that one idea.

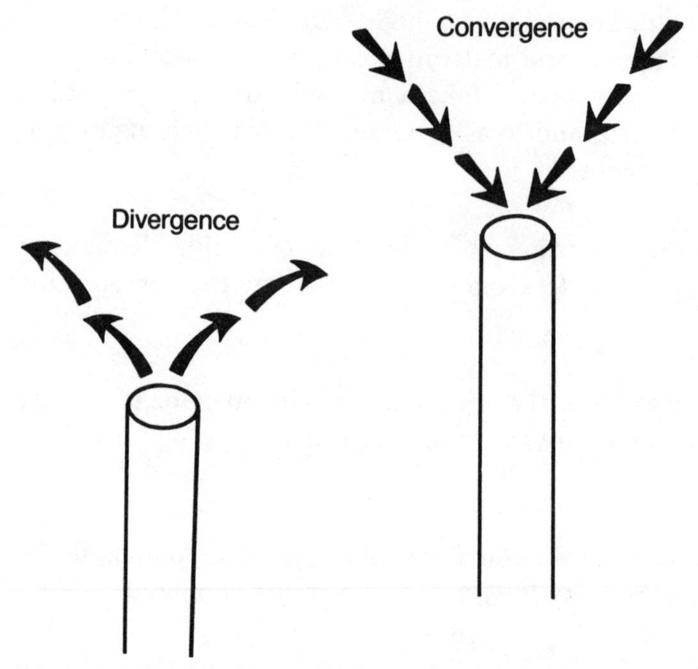

Figure 1 Diagram of divergence and convergence.

THE CREATIVE PROCESS

You've been looking at what creativity is and barriers to it. To bring the preceding concepts into focus look now at the creative process itself. Leslie Hart, author of *How the Brain Works,* says that since different people solve problems and seek opportunities in different ways, each brain builds on its own experience. We need to design work settings that are "brain-compatible, not brain-antagonistic." Mr. Hart believes that instead of emphasizing logical analysis of predigested facts, people should be encouraged to examine as much information as they can muster, consider a wide variety of approaches, and give their brains a chance to come up with a solution. "If we don't try to 'run the brain,'" Hart concludes, "this mighty instrument, more powerful than 100 large computers, will likely oblige us with excellent performance, making the best use of whatever experiences it has stored."

It is convenient to talk of the mind as if it were some information-handling machine, perhaps like a computer. The mind is not a machine, however, but a special environment which allows information to organize itself into patterns. The mind is very adept at making patterns. But to maximize opportunities, you must be willing to break patterns. As Eddie West, a Wilson Learning friend formerly of Milliken Textiles, once said, "You have to break a few eggs to make an omelette." This means generating new ideas. It means breaking out of the conceptual prisons of old ideas.

Remember that creativity is the process of breaking old connections and making novel and useful new connections—seeing relationships among things where you don't ordinarily see relationships. This is accomplished by following the creative process of generating alternatives and then evaluating them.

When generating alternatives, brainstorm as many ideas as possible without critiquing or judging them in any way. When evaluating alternatives, objectively judge them and combine the best ideas into a plan of action.

The key to the creative process is to keep generation distinct from evaluation.

When you attempt to accomplish both simultaneously, confusion is likely to occur, resulting in fewer creative ideas generated and a weaker plan of action. Before looking at the brainstorming process, however, it is important to look at just what you are going to brainstorm. What question will you try to answer?

Creative Problem Definition

You have probably been involved in a meeting where you defined a problem and proceeded to try to solve it. Often the process of defining the problem limits creative abilities. The following true story illustrates a creative problem definition.

A vegetable growers' association had a problem with damaged produce. They were especially concerned about the number of damaged tomatoes that were arriving at the market. The losses were intolerable, and they gathered together to develop a solution. They defined the problem as the question: How can we improve on the packaging of tomatoes? They brainstormed their own ideas and came up with some very good ideas. Though it was expensive, they chose to wrap each tomato separately. But the problem persisted. So they called in a consultant.

The consultant began by having them look at where they had limited their thinking. The first place they had done so was in how they defined the problem. He suggested that they generate alternative definitions of the problem. The definition the team finally settled on was: "How can we reduce the number of tomatoes arriving at market damaged?" This new definition was broader, left open more possibilities. This was in contrast to the first definition limiting them to looking at packaging.

Given the new definition, the solution they came up with and implemented was to develop a variety of tomatoes with thicker skins. They were unlikely to come up with this solution using their previous problem definition. Unfortunately, people do not always think about applying creativity to the problem-definition step. All too often people use their logical, analytical approach to get a factual definition and limit their creative thinking to the solution.

First, look at the problem as given. Begin the process of creatively defining the problem by writing a statement of the problem as given, for example, "How to better pack and ship tomatoes."

Second, analyze. Look at the problem from several angles using a series of questions such as: "What is the problem?" "Whose problem is it?" "What has been tried?" etc.

Third, spark creativity. Use questions to start the team thinking "outside the nine dots." Such questions might include: "How might we broaden the definition?" "How might we narrow the definition?" "How is this problem like other problems?"

Fourth, generate alternatives. List as many definitions of the problem as possible by completing the phrase: "How to . . . (Answering "how to" keeps people generating alternative definitions and out of generating alternative solutions.)

Fifth, select the definition that best reflects the nature of the problem.

Finally, continue the problem-solving process.

Another example of creative problem definition is given by Silver:

> Early on in the space race, NASA spent much time and effort seeking a metal robot strong enough to withstand the heat of reentry and protect the astronauts. The endeavor failed. At some point, a clever person changed the problem. The real problem was to protect the astronauts, and perhaps this could be done without a material that could withstand reentry. The solution, the ablative heat shield, had characteristics just opposite to those originally sought. Rather than withstanding the heat, it slowly burnt away and carried the heat away from the vehicle.

Having looked at how posing the question creatively reflects the problem, turn your attention to generating alternative answers to this question.

BRAINSTORMING

Generating alternatives, or what is commonly called brainstorming, is an essential technique for bringing out the creative talents of the team. Generating alternatives uses the collective mind of the group to produce a large quantity of ideas or possible solutions.

Each team member has a vast quantity and variety of ideas available at any given moment. Often this resource goes untapped. Using the dynamics of a group, you can create a flurry of activity into which individuals get swept up. The result is frequently the unleashing of the team's creativity. Consider what you have learned so far about overcoming limited thinking as well as ways to overcome limitations to participation. Overcoming these barriers is at the heart of the following guidelines for brainstorming.

Guidelines for Effective Brainstorming

Go for Quantity. While generating alternatives, the game is quantity not quality. Save the quality issue for the evaluation process.

Limit Time. Setting a time limit serves two purposes. First, it provides a subtle pressure which sparks people's motivation. This pressure allows people to shoot ideas out in an explosive, shotgun manner, without taking the time to stop and evaluate. The result is more ideas with greater variety. Second, setting a time limit keeps the team from taking up too much time generating ideas without leaving enough time to evaluate them. Brainstorming can be so much fun that people may not want to quit.

Free Wheeling. Share all ideas no matter how absurd they may seem. Piggyback off each other's ideas—use one idea to jar loose other ideas. Do not evaluate, judge, or criticize ideas at this point. Simply accept all ideas. While generating alternatives, there is no such thing as a bad idea.

Write It Down. Capture *all* ideas as they occur. Capture them when you can, for they tend to be illusive when trying to recollect them later. It is often useful to assign someone as a recorder responsible for writing the ideas down on paper.

The next two suggestions are much easier said than done, and they may not fit your management style. Nonetheless, they should be considered in any discussion of brainstorming.

Be Childlike. Children have the wonderful ability to express imagination, be spontaneous, and concentrate all at once. Just watch children at play. Inside each adult is a five-year-old genius waiting to come out—let the child out. Also be aware that childlike is *not* childish. Being childlike is constructive. Being childish is destructive. Childlike behavior encourages play and synergy among team members. Childish behavior discourages participation and creates hard feelings. Be aware of the difference, and be sensitive in your manner of adjusting the behavior. Whether you can be childlike or not, don't downplay this capability in members of your team.

Use Humor. Humor is a funny thing. It indicates the joyous, spontaneous connection of thoughts to form a pattern. One good way to judge the success of a brainstorming session is by how much laughter rings out.

Brainstorming sessions are one very effective way of breaking patterns. Perhaps the most common way of breaking patterns, however, is less structured, it happens "out of the blue" and is known as *insight.*

INSIGHT

Insight is that part of the creative process that appears the most mystical. It's the "out-of-the-blue" idea that leads many to believe that creativity "just sort of comes to you." Insight is simply illumination, as if suddenly an idea is captured in a spotlight. The creation of an insight follows a simple, easy-to-learn process.

The Insight Process

Step 1: Focus on the task. If your task is to solve a problem, really dive into it. Wholly involve your whole brain in the task. Recall the earlier definition of focused energy.

Step 2: Recreate. Even the word implies creativity: re-create. Take breaks in which you get completely away from the task. Exert yourself physically by taking a walk or running. Or just relax, read a book, meditate, tell jokes, break for lunch—any activity that distracts you from the task. This allows potential ideas to incubate until they're ready to hatch. Many people can identify the places they visit or the activities they engage in during which insights occur. It is important to take notice of these since that recognition facilitates the insight process.

Step 3: Oscillate. Go back and forth between focus and recreation. Continue this process, and be patient. Typically the idea will emerge as you switch from focus to recreation or from recreation to focus. Many good ideas occur to people just before sleep, while in the shower, while driving to work, and so on.

It is important to understand the process by which insights occur so that you can facilitate their occurrence in the work place. The transition back and forth between focusing and recreating is critical. For example, think about when your work unit is trying to solve a problem, the pressure is on to resolve the issue, and you're stuck. Typically the group will tend to respond by pushing harder, putting even more pressure on themselves. They find themselves saying things like: "We're not leaving until this is resolved," or "Come on, we're smart people; if we try harder and put our heads together, we can solve the problem."

This approach of keeping the pressure on, however, goes directly against the process for gaining insight. Insights are more likely to occur when people are relaxed, when their mental engines are idling. Biographers of Mozart claim his music almost wrote itself while he traveled or slept. Another example of "sleeping on it," occurred when Friedrich Kekule, a German chemist, fell asleep while trying to unravel the structure of the benzene molecule. While he slept he dreamed of atoms dancing around, forming shapes and patterns, twisting like snakes. Suddenly one snake grabbed its own tail and Kekule was hit with the insight that benzene has a closed-chain structure, an important scientific discovery.

Before leaving the topic of insights, think for a minute about what happens when you are talking with your boss and an insight hits you. How do you typically react? Most people do nothing; they try to hide the fact that it happened for fear it will appear as though they aren't paying attention. If this has happened to you, it's probably a fair assumption that it has happened to members of your work unit or team. Consider what it would be like to have a creative environment in which people felt free to talk about insights *when* they happen. The key here is that you need to create an environment in which members of your team feel they have permission to share the insights they get as they occur. If insights are slow in emerging, you might try to encourage them by using analogies.

ANALOGIES

One of the most difficult situations to deal with when a group is problem solving is when you become stuck. How you get unstuck is critical. One way to help you disconnect, generate alternatives, and then reconnect is by using analogies.

Analogies help you compare and contrast your topic to other worlds.

For example, the problem-solving process is analogous to an animal's metabolism:

Animal Metabolism	Problem-Solving Process
Search for and take in food	Search for and take in alternatives
Digest food	Break into component parts
Reassemble into new chemicals	Reassemble into new ideas
Evaluate what is useful and what is waste	Evaluate which ideas are useful and which aren't
Use energy to live and grow	Implement ideas

The point here is that there are many connections between seemingly disconnected worlds. If you can look for those connections, it may help you better solve your work-related problems. It was this connecting process that led Darwin to his natural selection evolutionary theory and Gutenberg to inventing the printing press.

Analogies have proven very useful—especially in problem solving. You may be thinking, "How am I going to use an analogy like that in the real world? People will think I'm crazy." Not necessarily. For example, here is a practical application of the use of analogies from the real world of packaging design. A major problem in packaging potato chips is that they are so fragile and susceptible to crushing that they are typically packed loose, thus requiring a great deal of shipping and shelf space for the package. In looking for an analogous situation, a problem-solving group came up with a similarity found in nature, one of the best resources of problem analogies:

Problem: Space required to pack fragile potato chips.
Analogy: Dry leaves, which are also very fragile.
Question: When *aren't* dry leaves fragile?
Answer: When they're *wet.*
Application: Pack potato chips in a much smaller package when they're wet, then dry them *in the package.*
Product: Pringle's potato chips in a tube.

Another real world problem faced by a group of product planners was how to help gardeners plant seeds at the correct intervals for proper plant spacing and growth:

Problem: Correct seed spacing.
Analogy question: What other multiple-unit items must be maintained at the correct distance apart in order to function properly?
Answer: Machine gun bullets.
Question: How do they maintain the correct distance?
Answer: At one time they were held together in a belt.
Application: Seeds sealed at the correct spacing in a water-soluble "belt," ready for planting.

A third example occurred long ago when a Shaker woman was sitting on her front porch working at her spinning wheel and watching two men sawing a log using a two-man saw. As she spun, the idea of a circular saw hit her. A more recent invention was born when a group from NASA was looking for a nonzipper fastener. Members of this group were going through a fantasizing exercise and one member visualized going through a jungle wearing flannel pants, and things began sticking to them. Observing this phenomenon led to the invention of Velcro.

The "other worlds" available from which to construct analogies are numerous, as illustrated in Figure 2.

Analogies might be helpful in answering questions about improving your team's performance, for example:

How can we increase communication in our work unit?

How can we get more work done?

How can we motivate our team?

How can we be more creative?

How can we improve __________ ?

If your problem was, "How can we motivate our team?" you might pick the world of physics. One item might be that

Social	Physical		Life
religion	engineering	dynamics	biology
politics	mathematics	gravitation	bacteria
communications	mechanics	liquids	botany
education	statistics	gases	medicine
economics	geometry	elastics	cells
games	energy	thermometry	psychology
history	calculus	heat	anthropology
industry	meteorology	radioactivity	mammals
law	geology	vibration	insects
literature	physics	electricity	fishes
music	chemistry	sound	birds
philosophy	magnets		archaeology

Figure 2 Other worlds—possible parallels.

there are universal laws of physics. One connection to your problem might be that there are also universal laws employees must follow. Then ask: "How does this connection help us solve our real problem?" Maybe you need to communicate with your people about the consequences of not following those universal rules.

IN SUMMARY

It is possible to structure a creative, problem-solving environment that knows how to break patterns and generate opinions; does not defeat itself by using killer phrases that stifle creative energy; that allows for creativity; and that supports, nurtures, and values insights.

Once the work-unit climate encourages creativity, everyone can become a problem solver. In this environment, all members of the work unit can bring their special abilities to create high performance. Everyone can be creative and proactive. This attitude involves, first, a refusal to accept rigid patterns and, second, an ability to put things together in a different way.

Once members of the work unit have a problem-solving attitude, they do not need to be told on what occasions to use it. High performance becomes the norm; it no longer has to be a process or technique but becomes a way of thinking about things with a willingness to share ideas. Once these key context issues are in place, where creativity and insight are the norm, you are ready to look more closely into problem solving and opportunity discovery, the focus of the next chapter.

THE CREATIVE TEAM IN ACTION

Consider how your team is currently performing on the attribute of creativity (Figure 3).

Phase	Characteristics	Possible Actions
Team: (81 to 100)	• Group members balance idea generation and idea evaluation. • Creativity, as well as immediate results, are rewarded. • Group members recognize and appreciate alternative approaches to problem-solving.	• Encourage members to look for the positive aspects of any idea. • Reinforce the expression of ideas and insights. • Encourage the consideration of individual differences in generating alternatives.
Group: (61 to 80)	• More time is spent evaluating rather than generating ideas. • Creativity is rewarded only when it produces immediate results. • Group members are hesitant to express new ideas or approaches.	• Encourage members to generate all possible options before evaluating the best. • Reinforce the creative process even when results are not immediate. • Facilitate nonjudgmental creativity sessions for the group.
Collection: (0 to 60)	• Members assume that their initial reactions are best. • Group members focus on the negative consequences of creative solutions. • Group meetings do not allow for creativity.	• Probe to discover ideas that may be less obvious. • Emphasize creativity as a process, rather than as an outcome. • Ask members for alternative approaches to problem solutions.

Figure 3 Use of creative talent—appreciating and applying individual skills.

Teams with low performance in this area show little recognition for members' unique skills and talents. Those with average performance indicate an appreciation for creativity, but little interest in learning another's skills or sharing their skills with others. In contrast, teams with superior performance make good use of their creative talent, openly share their skills, and learn from one another.

Opportunity—something more people would recognize if it didn't come disguised as hard work.
—Changing Times

An optimist sees an opportunity in every calamity; a pessimist sees a calamity in every opportunity.
—*Anonymous*

9

Rapid Response: What Opportunities Are Out There Waiting?

Ask Yourself . . .

- Are most decisions in your group achieved through consensus?
- Is the group bogged down in analytical problem-solving process?
- Is there a clear decision-making strategy and process?
- Do you focus on present problems or on future opportunities?
- How much time is spent reaching decisions?

The parents of ten-year-old twins requested the help of a psychologist. Although they treated both sons the same, one was extremely negative, constantly complaining; the other was extremely positive, to a fault. The psychologist agreed to work with the boys after observing them through a one-way window.

Mark, the pessimist, was put into the observation room which had been filled with goodies: candy, pop, electronic games of every description, craft materials, and a jukebox. Mark found fault with everything: the candy was too sweet, the pop wasn't cold enough, the electronic games were too easy, the crafts were too hard, and the jukebox had stupid records.

When Tim, the optimist, was put into the room, it was filled with nothing but piles of horse manure and a shovel. Eagerly, Tim began shoveling through the piles, commenting aloud, "With all this horse poop, there must be a pony in here somewhere."

In a work-related example, Silver tells a favorite story of Akio Morita, one of Sony Corporation's co-founders:

> Two shoe salesmen find themselves in a rustic backward part of Africa. The first salesman wires back to his head office: "There is no prospect of sales. Natives do not wear shoes!" The other salesman wires: "No one wears shoes here. We can dominate the market. Send all possible stock."

Or consider the experience of Frederick Smith who perceived a problem with the low reliability of airfreight and its high price. In a paper for an economics course at Yale University he proposed an airline to carry small packages from city to city overnight. This airline would have its own fleet of trucks and operate independently of all commercial airline flight schedules. Although he got a C on the paper, he remained undaunted and founded Federal Express Corporation.

OPTIMISTIC AND OPPORTUNISTIC

One characteristic that distinguishes those who make it to top management is how they deal with problems and opportunities. Formal management courses often teach students to solve problems posed in case studies or to identify opportunities for the organization based on certain market analyses. Such courses tend *not* to teach how to identify which problems need to be solved or how to exploit opportunities once they are recognized. Successful managers are those who anticipate problems before they become evident and who quickly exploit opportunities available to them.

In short, high-performance teams are *opportunistic.*

This chapter explores how to create teams that exhibit the attribute of *rapid response.* One way to develop this attribute is through a process developed by George Land called *Opportunity Discovery.*

THE OPPORTUNITY DISCOVERY PROCESS

To use this process, you first need a problem, either an existing problem or one you anticipate may arise in the future. For example, if no problem currently exists, you can use the creative talents of your team for planning, strategizing, and anticipating change.

You probably know entrepreneurs who intuitively know or recognize opportunities long before others. The Opportunity Discovery Process is a system you can use not only for solving existing problems, but also to identify future opportunities. The process allows a group to take advantage of its talents and also leads to commitment and responsibility for changes.

Opportunity Mapping consists of seven steps:

1. State the desired outcome.
2. Search for data.
3. Identify characteristics.
4. "Com-Pair" characteristics.
5. Rate existing performance.

6. Graph opportunities (opportunity mapping).
7. Create an Action Plan.

The following discussion illustrates each step in detail.

Step 1: Desired Outcome

Start by stating what you want to accomplish or have happen. For example, increase production 5 percent by the end of the fiscal year, have an information system in place by June 1, or have new salespeople producing X$ sales by the end of the first year.

To illustrate the Opportunity Discovery Process, consider the desired outcome to be: *Having a High-Performance team.* After all, that is the purpose of your reading this book.

Step 2: Search for Data

Next take stock of your current strengths and weaknesses related to the outcome. One of the most difficult, but necessary, actions is to examine the existing situation in regard to your desired outcome. You want to build off your strengths and work to overcome your weaknesses to accomplish the desired outcome.

This step is also important to getting the creative energy flowing and to building a data bank of potential ideas to choose from.

Based on what you know about creativity and generating alternatives, take a few minutes to identify your team's strengths and weaknesses as a high-performance team. You have been doing this on each attribute at the end of each chapter, so this step should be relatively easy for you to complete.

Step 3: Identify Characteristics

Based on the information you generated in Step 2, project into the future and assume you have accomplished your desired outcome. Identify the qualities or characteristics present that allowed you to accomplish the desired outcome. Do not list "how to's" at this point. That comes later during the Action Plan step. What you are looking for are the more global qualities or characteristics present.

Returning to the example, imagine it is a year from now and you have achieved your purpose—the team is performing better than you imagined. Think about what characteristics or qualities are present that allow you to say you have accomplished the outcome. One such characteristic might be high quality of communication within the team.

Step 4: "Com-Pair" Characteristics

Next you compare each characteristic to each other to determine the *priority* of every item. This is done by numbering each characteristic identified in Step 3 and looking at each characteristic compared to the other characteristics in the list (Figure 1).

Take your first two characteristics and ask yourself the following question: "It is a year from now and we have accomplished our desired outcome. We have all of these characteristics present. When com-paired, which of the two characteristics is more important?"

This is not an "either-or" choice. It is a comparison to establish which of any two qualities is more important. You are determining the *relative* importance of each characteristic.

Returning to the desired outcome of having a high-performance team, assume your first two characteristics are participative leadership (#1) and shared responsibility (#2). You must decide which of these two attributes is more important and circle its number. Say you feel #1 is more important, you'd circle that number like this:

(1) 1 1 1
2 3 4 5

										Value	Existing Performance
1	1	1	1	1	1	1	1	1	1	________	________
2	3	4	5	6	7	8	9	10			
	2	2	2	2	2	2	2	2	2	________	________
	3	4	5	6	7	8	9	10			
		3	3	3	3	3	3	3	3	________	________
		4	5	6	7	8	9	10			
			4	4	4	4	4	4	4	________	________
			5	6	7	8	9	10			
				5	5	5	5	5	5	________	________
				6	7	8	9	10			
					6	6	6	6	6	________	________
					7	8	9	10			
						7	7	7	7	________	________
						8	9	10			
							8	8	8	________	________
							9	10			
								9	9	________	________
								10			
									10	________	________

Figure 1 Com-pairing.

Next compare the first attribute (participative leadership) with the third attribute, perhaps being future-focused. If you feel being future-focused (#3) is more important than participative leadership (#1), your listing would now look like this:

① 2 3 4

2 ③ 4 5

After this, you compare the first attribute with the fourth through tenth attribute, or however many attributes you have.

When you have compared the first attribute with the other attributes, you look at the second attribute in the same way. You have already looked at #2 compared to #1, so you begin by comparing #2 with #3:

```
 2    2  2  2
(3)   4  5  6
```

If you have ten attributes, your comparison would look something like that in Figure 1.

In the example, highest priority is for item #9, lowest for item #2.

After you have made all of your "com-pair" choices, add up the number of times each item was circled. Be sure to look in each row and column to avoid missing any. You might want to check each one off as you count it. Once you have made your count for the number of times #1 was circled, put that figure in the column headed "Value." Do this for each characteristic. To be sure you have added correctly, the total should be 45 if you have 10 characteristics on your list (Figure 2).

This process is done individually; the scores are then combined in the group to arrive at a group score.

For example, your group may have written a mission statement and defined several specific goals which they must accomplish in line with that mission statement. Comparing could be used by the group to determine the order of priority for those goals. Comparing results can lead to an excellent discussion of the views of various individuals within the team and the importance they place on each of those goals.

Step 5: Rate Existing Performance

Once you have ranked each characteristic, rate how well you are currently performing with each. Return to the present, not one year out. It is important to be very honest and rate how

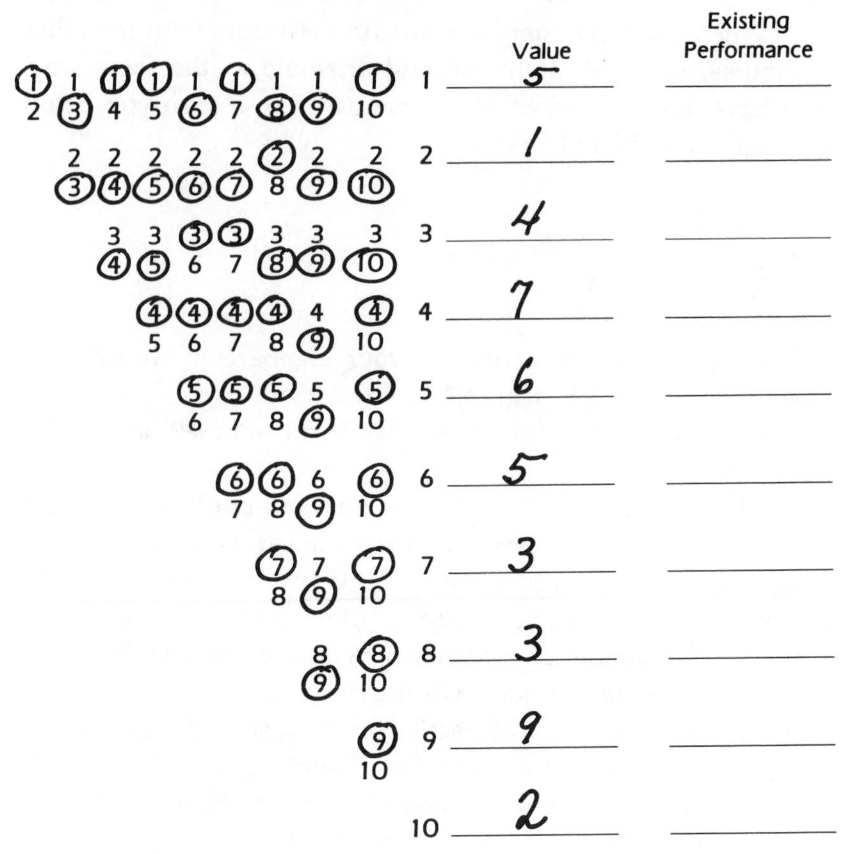

Figure 2 Com-pairing.

well you are *actually* doing, not how well you think you ought to be doing.

Determine on a scale from 0 to 100 how well these characteristics are presently being performed.

For example, if a characteristic is being done perfectly *now,* you'd give it a 100. If it isn't being done at all, or it is nonexistent, give it a zero. If it's just getting by, give it about 50. Rate each characteristic in terms of your assessment of existing performance.

When you have completed each of these steps, your page should look like Figure 3.

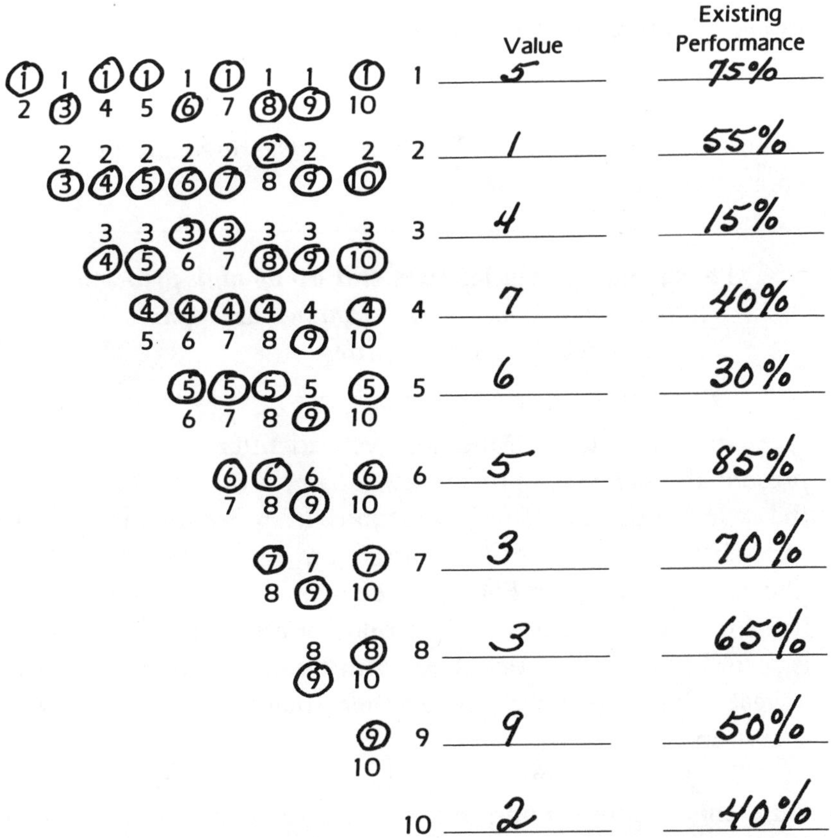

1 1 1 1 1 1 1 1 1
2 3 4 5 6 7 8 9 10

2 2 2 2 2 2 2 2
3 4 5 6 7 8 9 10

3 3 3 3 3 3 3
4 5 6 7 8 9 10

4 4 4 4 4 4
5 6 7 8 9 10

5 5 5 5 5
6 7 8 9 10

6 6 6 6
7 8 9 10

7 7 7
8 9 10

8 8
9 10

9
10

	Value	Existing Performance
1	5	75%
2	1	55%
3	4	15%
4	7	40%
5	6	30%
6	5	85%
7	3	70%
8	3	65%
9	9	50%
10	2	40%

Figure 3 Com-pairing.

Again, you do this individually first. To arrive at a group score, take an average. That is, start with item #1 and have each person share what he or she has as a number for this characteristic. Add up these numbers and divide by the number of individuals in the group. If you have six individuals in the group and the following numbers: 65, 70, 55, 70, 60, and 50, you'd add these figures to arrive at 370. Divide 370 by 6 (number of individual scores) for an average rating of 62. (Round figures to the nearest whole number.)

Continue with this process for the remaining characteristics.

Step 6: Graph Opportunities (Opportunity Mapping)

Now take your priority and performance ratings and plot them on a graph.

Those characteristics that end up as *high priority,* and *low existing performance* are your *opportunities.*

An Opportunity Map lets you identify areas that will present the greatest opportunity for improvement in reaching the desired outcome. The Opportunity Map has the rating scale for Existing Performance running from right (100) to left (0). The average Existing Performance scores are plotted on this line for each characteristic. The value or attribute priority scale is recorded on the vertical line, with ten as highest and one as lowest. When these are put together, they look like the profile shown in Figure 4.

To plot the score, using the preceding example, begin with the "Value" rating for characteristic #1 and move a marker *up* the center vertical line until you come to the correct value for that item.

From this point, move *across* the horizontal line (either right or left) to locate the percentage of "Existing Performance" for characteristic #1. Place a dot at this point and label it Point 1.

Repeat this process for each characteristic using the "Value" and "Existing Performance" ratings. When you are finished, your Opportunity Map should be like that in Figure 5.

After plotting your scores, you are ready to interpret them. Notice that the Opportunity Profile is divided into four quadrants, each with a specific meaning.

Upper-Left Quadrant—Satisfiers. Items in this quadrant are important to you, but you are presently doing well, relative

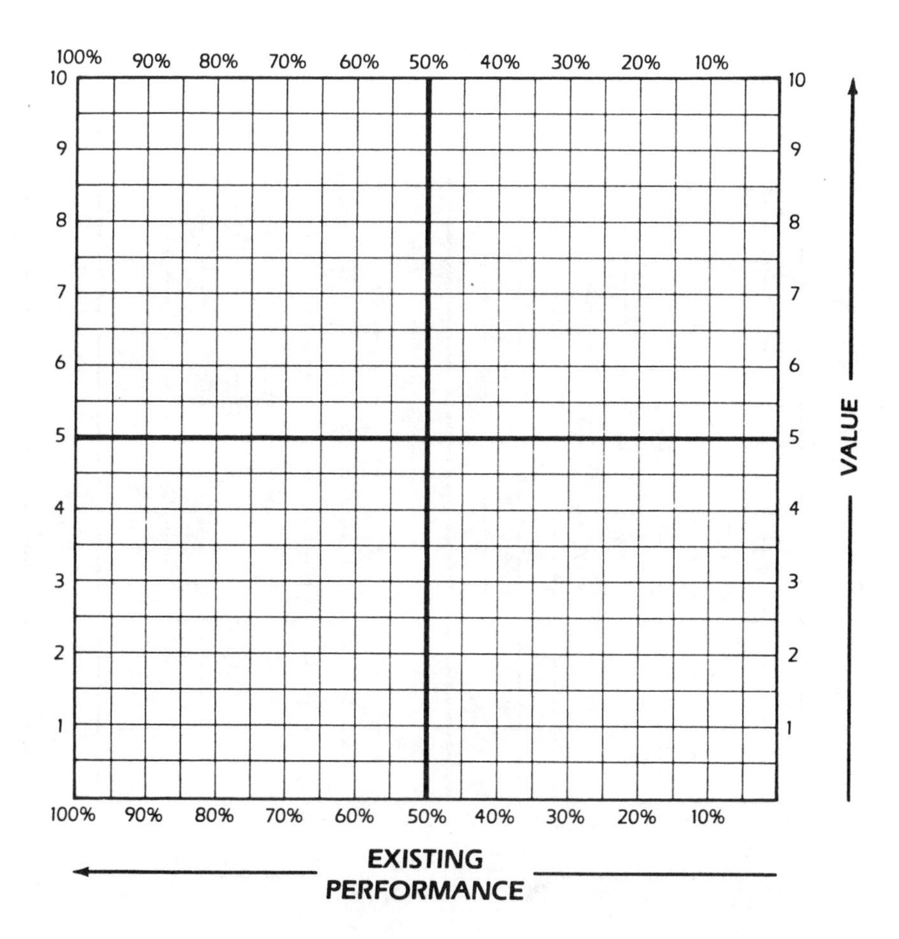

Figure 4 The opportunity profile.

to the other characteristics. Therefore, they are *satisfiers.* You probably want to maintain these characteristics and keep them happening.

Lower-Left Quadrant—Overkills. These are characteristics that are low in value, but high in performance. You may be spending too much time/energy here and may need to focus some of these energies elsewhere.

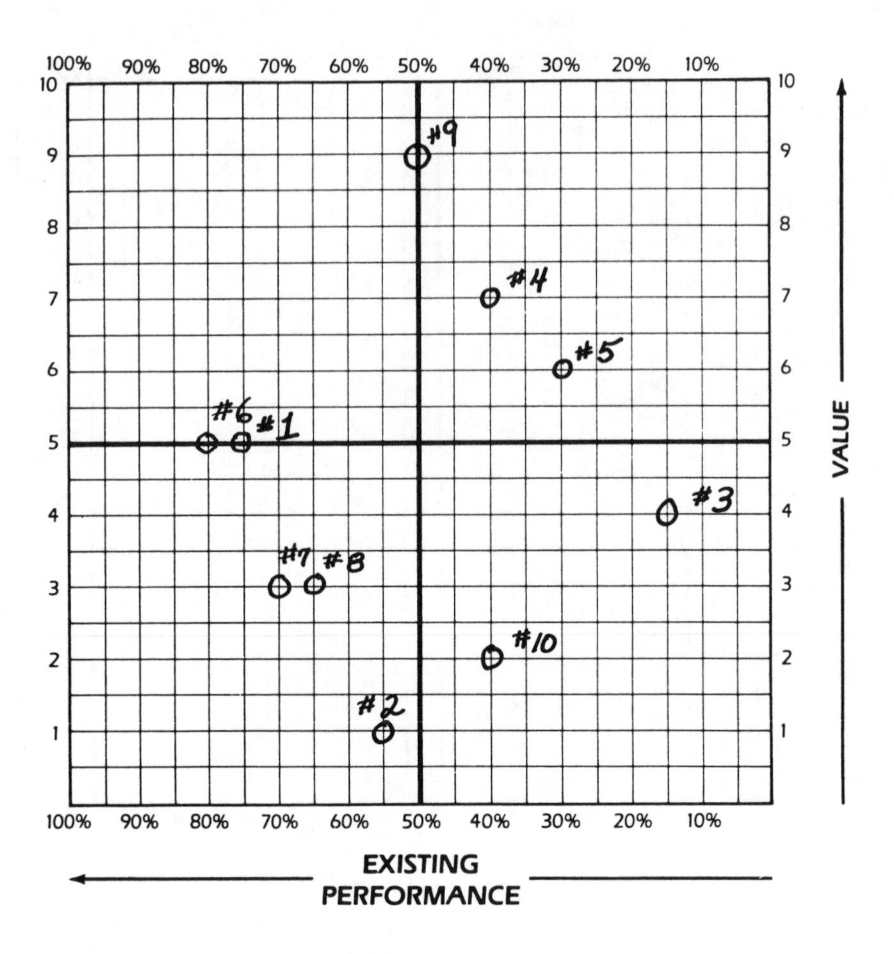

Figure 5 The opportunity profile.

Lower-Right Quadrant—Gripes. These characteristics are low in priority and low in performance. People like to talk about gripes, but in reality they are not priorities for change. It could be they really aren't gripes, but, relative to other characteristics, are lower in priority. Nevertheless, people may expend energies griping rather than performing creatively. This may be an area where you can redirect energy.

Upper-Right Quadrant—Opportunities. These characteristics are high in value, but low in performance. They are your *opportunities,* areas you will want to focus your energies to see that the desired result (in this case the high-performing team) is accomplished.

Opportunity Mapping can be used for nearly any problem *if* you have a fairly clear idea of what the desired end result is.

Step 7: Create an Action Plan

The last step is to establish the "how to's" for the characteristics you have identified as opportunities, all the Who? What? Where? When? How? information that is critical to create an Action Plan. Use the Plan of Action Chart illustrated in Figure 6.

What. Given the action steps generated by the large group, select one or more that you wish to implement in your work unit. Write these under "What" in the preceding chart.

Who. Next to each "What," write the name of the person who will complete this action. (If the person is you, write "me.")

How. Under "How," list the specific method(s) and/or materials needed to accomplish the "What."

Where. Under "Where," specify the location in which the "What" is to take place.

When. Under "When," commit to a specific time and due date by which you intend to accomplish the "What."

In Summary

The Opportunity Discovery Process involves the following seven steps:

PLAN OF ACTION

WHAT?	WHO?	HOW?	WHERE?	WHEN?

Figure 6 Plan of action chart.

1. State desired outcome.
2. Search for data.
3. Identify characteristics.
4. Rate existing performance.
5. "Com-Pair" characteristics.
6. Graph opportunities (opportunity mapping).
7. Create an action plan.

A CREATIVE PROBLEM-SOLVING PROCESS

The Creative Problem-Solving Process can be used by your team to develop an Action Plan to solve a problem. This process has eight steps:

1. State the problem.
2. Identify the symptoms.
   —What information is possible to obtain?
3. Gather and share information.
   —What information is needed?
4. Define the problem.
   —What are possible definitions of the problem?
   —Which possible definitions are most important?
5. Generate ideas for solving the problem.
   —What are some ideas for possible solutions?
   —Which ideas do we like the best?
6. Evaluate ideas for solving the problem.
   —Is this particular idea effective?
   —Is this particular idea practical?
   —What are the most important criteria for an acceptable solution?
7. Combine ideas to build a solution.
   —What are possible solutions that fit the criteria?
   —Which solutions do we want?
8. Develop a plan to implement the solution.
   —Who? What? Where? When? How?

Notice that the Creative Problem-Solving Process includes both divergent and convergent thinking, as did the Opportunity Mapping Process.

A variety of problem-solving approaches are available. Each has a number of steps, but typically each involves four phases:

Phase I:	Defining the Problem (Steps 1–4)
Phase II:	Generating Possible Solutions (Step 5)
Phase III:	Evaluating Solutions (Step 6)
Phase IV:	Creating an Action Plan (Steps 7–8)

Each phase of problem solving is distinct and calls for distinctly different behavior from the team leader. Following are some *do's* and *don'ts* for each phase of problem solving.

Steps 1–4: Defining the Problem: Gathering Facts

DO'S:

- Do provide the pertinent data that you possess.
- Do provide the background context for the problem.
- Do explain how this problem relates to other departments.
- Do ask the group for whatever facts and data they possess.
- Do make sure that everyone understands all the facts and data.
- Do restate the definition of the problem to ensure that all members are aware of what you've got and what you want.

DON'TS:

- Don't allow the group to discuss solutions.
- Don't allow people to blame or assess faults regarding the problem.

- Don't move on in the process until everyone is clear about the definition of the problem.
- Don't supply them with irrelevant information.
- Don't act as though you have already decided on a solution and involving the team is merely a formality.

Step 5: Generating Possible Solutions

DO'S:

- Do encourage "off the wall" comments.
- Do challenge the group to push for as many possible solutions as they can think of.
- Do prime the pump with a *few* of your own ideas, especially if the group is stuck.
- Do set a time limit.
- Do invite everyone to participate, even if you have to call on them.
- Do ask open-ended questions to spark the team's thinking.
- Do write down *all* ideas generated.
- Do assure the team that all ideas are welcome, and that no idea is silly.
- Do piggyback off each other's ideas.

DON'TS:

- Don't allow editing, evaluating, or criticizing of ideas.
- Don't settle on the first "good" idea that surfaces.
- Don't punish members who criticize ideas—just remind them of the ground rules.
- Don't spend much time advocating your ideas.
- Don't dote over one person or one good idea.
- Don't go beyond time limits set unless the team wants to.
- Don't quit until the time limit is up.

Step 6: Evaluating Solutions

DO'S:

- Do review all the items on the list of possible solutions and eliminate those with no support.
- Do keep any item on the list that *anyone* is willing to discuss.
- Do focus the group on looking at the positive and negative aspects of each solution.
- Do anticipate the consequences of each solution.
- Do make sure that each member has ample opportunity to provide their input.
- Do invite members to combine solutions.
- Do ensure consensus by getting everyone's input.
- Do frequently restate what you hear to clarify the meaning.

DON'TS:

- Don't allow the team to judge each other as they judge the ideas.
- Don't get bogged down discussing the pros and cons—assess value quickly.
- Don't quit until you have clear consensus.

Steps 7–8: Creating an Action Plan

DO'S:

- Do generate alternative how-to's for implementation before choosing an Action Plan.
- Do make sure that specific tasks are assigned.
- Do involve the team in deciding who will do what.
- Do make sure that time frames are set.

- Do empower the members with the authority to complete their tasks.
- Do arrange a method of following up to ensure completion of the tasks.
- Do include yourself as a person responsible for a task.
- Do restate each member's role to clarify and ensure commitment.

DON'TS:

- Don't state roles and tasks in general, unmeasurable terms.
- Don't assume that brilliant solutions produce brilliant Action Plans—be creative in your planning.
- Don't forget to follow up.

In Summary

Figure 7 summarizes the problem-solving process.

THE OPPORTUNISTIC TEAM IN ACTION

How rapidly does your team recognize and respond to opportunities? (See Figure 8.)

Teams who are low on this attribute tend to solve problems on an "as need arises" basis, consensus takes long, and few leaders feel competent to make decisions.

Teams who are average on this attribute can anticipate problems, but are unable to respond rapidly to prevent further problems. In contrast, teams with high ability in this area set priorities rapidly and can anticipate and problem solve before the situation becomes a major problem. High-performing teams have well-worked-out problem-solving strategies; they are opportunistic.

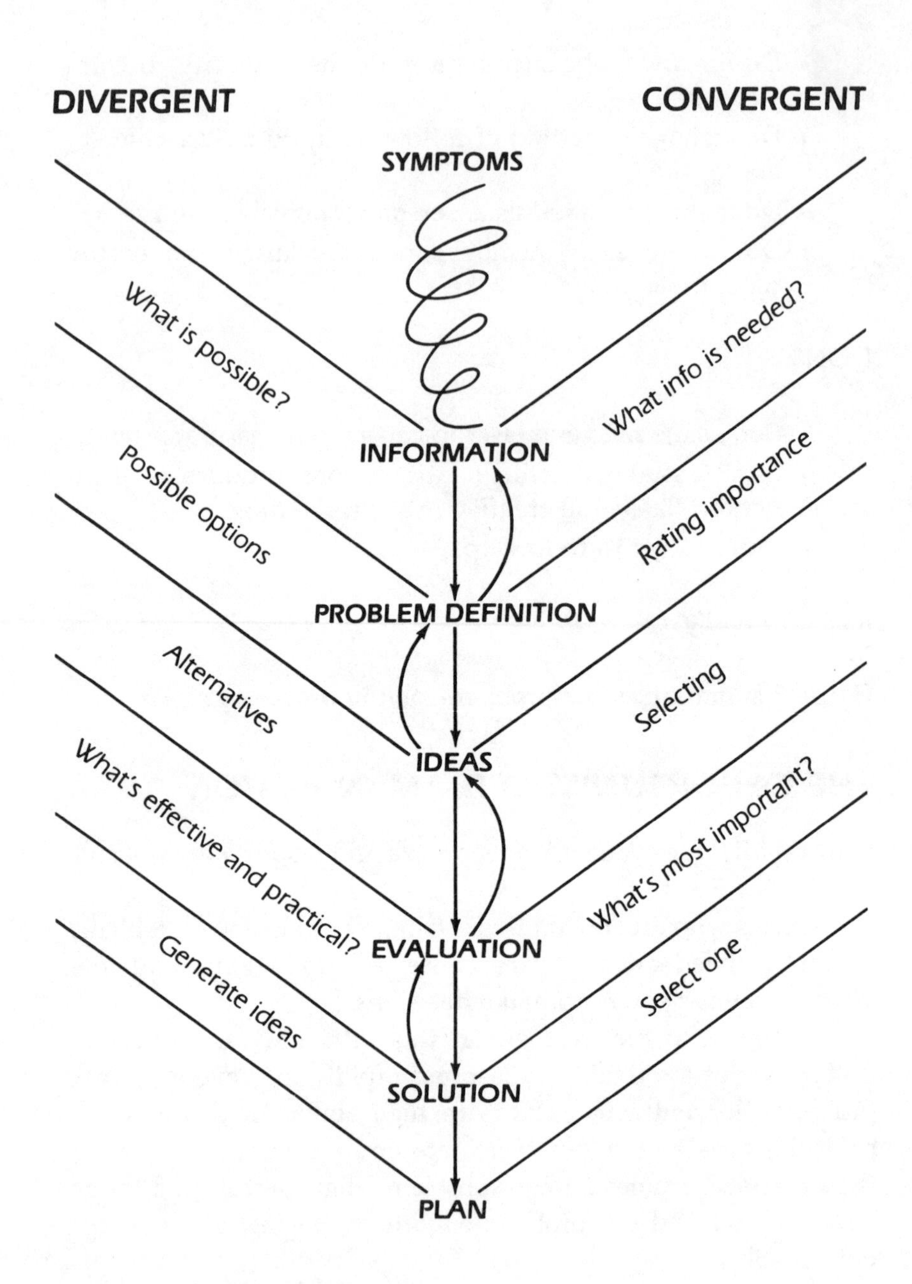

Figure 7 Problem-solving process.

Phase	Characteristics	Possible Actions
Team: (81 to 100)	• Group decisions are guided by an agreed-upon strategy and process. • Most decisions are achieved through consensus.	• Continue to reference the group strategy and process and revise it when necessary. • Reinforce consensus decision-making.
Group: (61 to 80)	• A strategy and process for decision-making is developed. • Decisions are often made by the leader and those with influence.	• Assure that members use the process and participate in modifying it. • Encourage all members to express their opinions and participate in decision-making.
Collection: (0 to 60)	• No clear decision-making process exists. • Decisions are typically made without group involvement.	• Facilitate the development of a strategy and process for group decision-making. • Involve group members in the decision-making process.

Figure 8 Rapid response—identifying and acting on opportunities.

Faith is to believe what we do not see; and the reward of this faith is to see what we believe.

—*St. Augustine*

The future, something everyone reaches at the rate of sixty minutes an hour, whatever he does, whoever he is.

—*C.S. Lewis*

10

Synergism: Making It Work

Ask Yourself . . .

- Can you pull together all you've learned and create a high-performance team?
- What is in your favor?
- What might stand in your way?

As a divorced mother with three children, Mary Kay Ash took her life savings of $5,000 and created a company worth hundres of millions. Silver describes how she accomplished this feat:

> She created a feeling of family in her company, a hierarchical organization which had a system of rewards and penalties,

like any family. Through frequent seminars attended by the independent beauty consultants, Ash "preaches" to her women like a tent-meeting evangelist. Typical of her gospel are the following precepts:

> If you are here today, you are too smart to go home and scrub floors. You are spending one dollar time on a one penny chore. . . . I created this company for you.

IT'S TIME TO IMPLEMENT

You've come a long way in learning about creating and managing high-performance teams. You've looked at examples of high performance teams, analyzed the various attributes of these teams, and learned about building skills necessary to acquire each attribute.

This chapter reviews the attributes of a high-performance team and then presents some options available to you for applying what you've learned to your job.

Harland Cleveland, noted author and lecturer on the subject of strategic thinking, stated: "Those who act, whatever their corner of the great complexity, must give unremitting attention to the 'whole' in order to act relevantly on their own part of it."

EIGHT ATTRIBUTES OF HIGH-PERFORMANCE TEAMS

High-performance teams are superior in eight attributes:

Participative Leadership: creating an interdependency by empowering, freeing up, and serving others

Shared Responsibility: establishing an environment in which all team members feel as responsible as the manager for the performance of the work unit

Aligned on Purpose: having a sense of common purpose as to why the team exists and the function it serves

High Communication: creating a climate of trust and open, honest communication

Future Focused: seeing change as an opportunity for growth

Focused on Task: keeping meetings focused on results and sharing responsibility for the meetings

Creative Talents: removing barriers to creativity and applying individual talents and skills creatively

Rapid Response: identifying and acting on opportunities.

Examples of these attributes are all around you. The intent of this book is to help you make them more a part of your team. The Opportunity Mapping you did should identify what attributes you need to focus on to create a high-performing team. Share this information with your team.

The team can then act as significant resources to each other to help each other change and sustain this change.

CREATING THE HIGH-PERFORMANCE TEAM

If your purpose is to create and manage a high-performance team, you must be personally *aligned on this purpose.* And you may need to change some of your traditional assumptions. You may need to shift from thinking about lower-level to higher-level management thinking, from thinking one-to-one to one-to-group, from authoritative leadership to participative leadership, and so on. And you may need to take some risks.

Maccoby (*The Gamesman*) used extended interviews, questionnaires, and psychological testing on 250 top management personnel in 12 high technology, multinational United States corporations and found that what he called "The Gamesman" was most likely to be in the top leadership roles in the corporate world:

> *The gamesman*—is challenged by strong competition [challenges] and winning over it, enjoys technological advances, wants to be

a winner, likes to take risks and motivates others, is a team player for the corporation. The contest hypes him up and he communicates his enthusiasm thus energizing others.

ACKNOWLEDGING STRENGTHS

One other area of thinking to examine is how you look at your own and your team member's strengths. When you're dealing with machines or objects, it's natural to look for what's wrong with them and make the necessary changes. The problem is that when you're dealing with humans, if all you look for are negatives, that will certainly affect the way you feel about yourself and your team members. Those feelings may become barriers to making the necessary changes to become a high-performance team.

High-performance teams recognize and acknowledge each other's strengths.

Why don't managers do a better job of acknowledging their own strengths and those of their team members? Perhaps because they were taught not to brag, they didn't want to embarrass others, or they were trained to look for negatives.

To succeed in making the shifts necessary to create high-performing teams and sustain change, one important shift is from looking at the negatives to looking for the positives. People need to feel their contribution is important. A poignant example of this is the lady who ran a loom in a textile factory for her entire working life. When she retired at age 65, she received a letter saying how valuable she'd been to the company, and she broke down in tears. She confided that it was the first time anyone had ever said something positive to her about her work there.

When time permits, take a sheet of paper and write down all your own work-related strengths. Make a similar listing for each member of your work unit. Share the lists with each of your team members privately.

To create a high-performance team, shift your thinking away from looking at negatives to looking at (and for) positives.

Positives are there, but it's usually a question of not looking for them. If you don't look for them, you usually don't acknowledge them to each other.

Part of the intent of creating a high-performance team goes beyond getting people to change and to choose to put forth more energy toward their job. It is to get them to feel good about themselves and each other. Shifting your focus to acknowledging strengths will help the process.

Harland Cleveland has outlined five capacities needed for effective leadership:

FIVE CAPACITIES REQUIRED FOR LEADERSHIP

1. The capacity to understand the context of one's own actions.
2. The capacity to do something rather than just to be someone.
3. The capacity to take initiative, a feeling that it is always "my turn," a sense of personal responsibility for change, a belief in the possibility of a change before it has actually happened.
4. The capacity to encourage and enhance supportive relationships among people, facilitate group decision-making and the sharing of responsibility.
5. The capacity to educate; to intervene to modify what people want as well as what institutions will accept.

YOU AS A TEAM MEMBER

So far you have focused on looking at your work unit and at how you can help make its members into a high-performance team. Think for a few minutes about your boss and your role as a member of his or her team. You probably share responsibility with other managers in your business or organization. Do you compete? Cooperate? Or collaborate? Are each of you independent or interdependent? Do you accept responsibility for what happens in your boss's meetings?

Thomas Quick describes what can happen when departments do not collaborate:

> A bank officer whose jurisdiction includes customer relations noted a significant increase in complaints of inaccuracies in the records of new customers that seemed attributable to computer errors. So she suggested that members of her staff hold a meeting with representatives of the operations department to talk about the increased customer complaints. But the meeting was a dismal failure. Her assistant described his reaction. "They were all over the place, even criticizing the quality of the customer contact people who are being hired. I just couldn't see how that kind of thing helps, and I told them so."
>
> The chief representative of the operations group had a different interpretation. "They kept saying that we should leave no stone unturned, anything we wanted to mention that could help the situation, fine. So we brought up a couple of ideas, and they started getting defensive as hell. I don't think we accomplished anything but raise more dust."
>
> What happened was that, after she outlined the major problems and complaints, the customer relations manager said, "I'm open to any suggestions." She said it two or three times. The other group accepted the invitation at face value—and ran into a hornet's nest.
>
> There were at least two major problems. The first had to do with the high turnover of people who sat behind the desks in lobbies of branch banks. They were not well paid, and tended to leave when their dissatisfaction reached intolerable levels. The other problem was caused in part by the proliferation of checking and savings plans brought about by competitive pressures. The variety of forms used introduced more opportunities for errors, especially among new reps. The operations people suggested more careful training. But when

they suggested this solution, the customer relations manager became angry and complained that the discussion was going off on a tangent.

Actually, she had been sincere in saying she wanted an open discussion. She had determined to her satisfaction where the fault lay—in the operations department itself.

In this instance the departments' tasks were interdependent, but they were not working as a team. The customer relations manager was concentrating on proving her position right rather than on creatively and collaboratively solving the problem. Managers might take a lesson from Albert Einstein, who at the height of his fame was asked by a reporter: "How do you feel, knowing that so many people are trying to prove that you are not right?" The great scientist replied: "I have no interest in being right. I'm only concerned with discovering whether I am or not."

PLANS FOR CHANGE

You've covered a lot of material. The big question now is what you intend to do with it. You may sit back and wait for others to change and look at how you might implement some of the ideas you have learned. On the other hand, you may take the initiative and view it as your turn.

Since taking the first step is sometimes the most difficult, this book concludes by asking a few questions to help you with that first step.

Take a few minutes to look at your Opportunity Mapping and your Action Plan Guide. Now consider:

- What are *you* going to do?
- What is your intention?

Don't try to do everything at once. Focus. Look at your Opportunity Map and select the one attribute that will help your team most to develop. Then, in the box below, write down one thing you want to change as a result of reading this book (Figure 1).

You now have the knowledge necessary to create a high-performance team. You also know how to develop the skills required of such a team. It is hoped that you also have changed some assumptions about managing/leading your work unit—that you have a positive attitude toward being a participative leader, for using a one-to-group approach when appropriate, and for sharing responsibility for your work unit's successes and failures. The challenge is to put into practice what you have learned.

Figure 1.

PLANS FOR CHANGE

List three steps you are willing to take to begin to implement what you have learned.

Phrase your statements as follows:

As a result of Creating the High-Performance Team, I am going to . . .

1. ______________________________

____

____

2.

3.

References

Bennis, Warren and Nanus, Burt. *Leaders: The Strategies for Taking Charge.* New York: Harper and Row, Publishers. 1985.

Burns, James MacCregor. *Leadership.* New York: Harper & Row, 1978.

Cohen, Allan and Bradford, David. *Managing for Excellence.* New York: John Wiley & Sons, Inc., 1984.

Garfield, Charles A. *Peak Performers: The New Heroes of American Business.* New York: William Morrow & Co., Inc., 1986.

Geneen, Harold. *Managing.* New York: Doubleday. 1985.

Maccoby, Michael. *The Gamesman.* New York: Simon and Schuster, 1976, p.285.

McGinnis, Alan Loy. *Bringing Out the Best in People.* Minneapolis, MN: Augsburg Publishing House, 1985.

Oberg, Mary. *Whole Brain Learning Project.* Funded by the Minnesota Council on Quality Education. Minneapolis: Minneapolis Public Schools, 1985.

Quick, Thomas L. *An Executive's Guide to Working Effectively with People: Person to Person Managing.* New York: St. Martin's Press, 1977.

Silver, A. David. *Entrepreneurial Megabucks: The 100 Greatest Entrepreneurs of the Last Twenty-Five Years.* New York: John Wiley & Sons, 1985.

Spring, Sally and Deutsch, George. *Left Brain/Right Brain.* San Francisco: W. H. Freeman, 1981, p.192.

Watkin, Edward. "Management Strategy: Tackle Those Goals!" *Today's Office,* September, 1985, pp.48–50.

Zenger, John H. "Leadership: Management's Better Half," *Training,* December, 1985, p.48.

APPENDIX A

MEETING CHECKLIST

Item	Complete/Status
1. Participants informed of time and place of meeting?	
2. Purpose and agenda prepared?	
3. Anticipating potential problems?	
4. Meeting room reserved?	
5. Meeting room prepared?	
a. Right size for group	
b. Enough tables and chairs	
c. Tables and chairs properly arranged	

Item	Complete/Status
d. Ashtrays or "no-smoking" signs, as appropriate	
e. Refreshments (if desired)	
6. Necessary visual aids equipment reserved?	
a. Flipchart	
b. Blackboard	
c. Overhead projector	
d. Movie projector	
e. Video recorder/monitor	
7. Visual aids equipment set up?	
8. Material for visual aids prepared?	
a. Overlays	
b. Key points written on flipchart	
c. Video cartridge/movie reserved	
9. Working condition of equipment checked out?	

Item	Complete/Status
10. Understanding of how to run equipment checked out?	
11. Handouts prepared?	
12. Supplies provided?	
a. Markers	
b. Paper, pencils/pens	
c. Tape/pins	
d. Name tags	

* * *

APPENDIX B

MECHANICS AND MATERIALS

I. Meeting Room

  A. Do you need an office or a conference room?

  B. Have you reserved a conference room?

    1. Who do you reserve it with?
    2. Is it accessible to all participants?
    3. Do all participants know where it is?

  C. Meeting Room Size

    1. Is it large enough for the group to be comfortable?
    2. Is it too big if you have a small group?

  D. Seating Arrangement

    1. Are there enough chairs and tables?
    2. What is the best arrangement? Take into account the following:

      a. Participation
      b. Good view of visual aids

  E. Working Materials

    1. Felt-tip pens
    2. Note pads

3. Pens/pencils
4. Name tags
5. Tape/pins

F. Lighting

1. Is the room light enough for normal use?
2. Is it dark enough for projection use yet light enough for participants to take notes?

G. Room Temperature

1. Body heat will raise the temperature; you may want to keep the room cooler.
2. Periodically check with the participants to see if they are comfortable. If you are up and moving, you may feel differently about the comfort level.

H. Smoking

1. If smoking is allowed, provide ashtrays.
2. If smoking is not allowed, you may want to include "no-smoking" signs.

II. Visual Aids

A. What visual aids are appropriate/available to you?

1. Flipchart

a. Write legibly.
b. Use felt-tip pens.
c. Write large enough so people in the back of the room can read what you write.
d. Leave plenty of space between lines.
e. Use different colors for emphasis.
f. Ensure there is enough paper.

2. Overhead projector

a. Set up projector near speaker, allowing speaker to face the group.
b. Set up projector far enough away from screen so that lettering or numbers are visible at the back of the room.

c. Arrange projector so everyone can see both screen and speaker. It is recommended you set the overhead projector in the middle of the front of the room with it angled to project on a screen in one of the front corners.
d. You may want to prepare transparencies with frames for ease of handling. (Remember, you may write notes to yourself on the frame, since no one will be able to see them.)
e. Use special pens to write on transparencies.
f. You may want to use a pointer to highlight key points. Point directly to transparency—not the screen—to avoid blocking anyone's view.

3. Movie projector
   a. Check film for breaks.
   b. Thread film properly to remove flutter.
   c. Focus lens.
   d. Set projector at proper distance so that it fills the screen.
   e. Adjust sound level and tone.

4. Video recorder and monitor
   a. Be sure the videotape format and size matches the machine.
   b. Check meter counter readings in case you want to find specific spots.
   c. Adjust brightness, contrast, color, etc., on monitor.

5. Blackboard
   a. Be sure you start with a clean board.
   b. Have chalk available, including spare pieces.
   c. Have erasers or wiping cloths available.
   d. Use colored chalk for emphasis.

B. Do you have to reserve any of the equipment?

   1. With whom do you reserve it?

C. Do you have to prepare any material for the visual aids?

   1. Writing key points on flipchart
   2. Preparing overlays for overhead projector
   3. Obtaining video cartridges for video presentation
   4. Reserving movies

D. Do you know how to run the equipment?

   1. Whom do you need to contact for help?
   2. Does the particular piece of equipment you have obtained operate any differently than what you are used to?

E. Is the equipment in working order?

   1. Plugs, light bulbs, switches, etc.?
   2. Have you actually tried it out to be sure?

III. Who Should Attend

A. Limit participants to only those who need to be there. (The more nonessential people attending, the higher the probability the meeting will go off task.)

B. If it is an information-sharing meeting, include:

   1. Those who need to know.
   2. Those whose input/feedback you want.
   3. Those most affected by the information.

C. If it is a problem-solving meeting, include:

   1. Those whose input you want.
   2. Those who have the **ability** to solve the problem.
   3. Those who have the **responsibility** to initiate/carry out the solution.

D. If you have guests:

   1. Allow time for introductions.
   2. Provide name tags.
   3. Present a brief summary of things you have covered to bring guests up to speed.

IV. Handouts

A. Use handouts to emphasize key points.

B. Use handouts that match overlays or prepared flipcharts.

C. Send handouts to participants in advance, so they can preview the information.

D. Use handouts if people will need information for discussion during meeting.

E. Use handouts so people leave the meeting with material to review for the next meeting.

Index

Creating the High-Performance Team Training Program

Wilson Learning Corporation has developed a training program based on the concepts in *Creating the High-Performance Team*, using both video and workbook material. This program is designed for in-house use in a workshop format, and has been used successfully in corporations and organizations across the United States.

For more information, fill out and return the card below.

Creating the High-Performance Team **Training Program**

Please send me further information on the
Creating the High-Performance Team
Training Program from Wilson Learning Corporation.

Name____________________

Title____________________

Company____________________

Address____________________

City, State, Zip____________________

No Postage
Necessary
If Mailed in the
United States

BUSINESS REPLY MAIL
FIRST CLASS MAIL Permit No. 1147 Hopkins, MN

Postage Will Be Paid by Addressee

Corporate Services
Wilson Learning
6950 Washington Ave., So.
Eden Prairie, Minnesota 55344-9948